Make Money Now Copywriting in Your Spare Time

Earn While You Learn Copywriting on Textbroker

By Casey Bahr

© 2016 by Casey Bahr. All rights reserved.

No part of this book may be reproduced in any written, electronic, recording, or photocopying without written permission of the publisher or author. The exception would be in the case of brief quotations embodied in the critical articles or reviews and pages where permission is specifically granted by the publisher or author.

Although every precaution has been taken to verify the accuracy of the information contained herein, the author and publisher assume no responsibility for any errors or omissions. No liability is assumed for damages that may result from the use of information contained within.

Book cover image © 2016 by Sean A. Bahr. All Rights Reserved. The image may not be reproduced in any written, electronic, recording, or photocopying without written permission of the artist.

Other images are open domain, non-attribution use.

Table of Contents

Chapter 1 - What You Will Learn from This Book 1
    Getting the Most from This Book in the Shortest Time Possible 2

Chapter 2 – QUICK START GUIDE 3
    Chapter Overviews 3

Chapter 3 - Introduction to Copywriting 5
    What is Copywriting? 5
    Types of Copy You May Write 5

Chapter 4 - The Benefits of Copywriting as a Job/Career 8
    Do You Like to Write? 8
    How You Make Money Copywriting 8
    What You Need to be Successful at Copywriting 9

Chapter 5 - Why Write on Textbroker? 11
    Bare Minimum of Marketing Required 11
    Superb Learning Platform 11
    Increasing Flow of Work 12
    Guaranteed Payment without a Middle Man 12
    Textbroker Drawbacks 13
    Is Textbroker's Commission Too High? 14

Chapter 6 - Getting Started on Textbroker 16
    Account Setup 16
    Your Textbroker Profile 20
    The Bottom Line with Your Profile 25

Chapter 7 – Textbroker Terms of Service (Do Not Skip!) 26
    Accepting the Textbroker Terms of Service 26
    One More Big (Actually Huge!) No-No: Plagiarism 29

Chapter 8 – Deciphering TB Orders 31

Order Types 31
Writer Star Levels Explained 32
Open Orders 32
Open Order Visual Anatomy 34
The 10-Minute Open Order Timer 38
Client Briefing 39
Things to Look Out for Before Accepting an Open Order 39

Chapter 9 – Unlocking the Mysteries of Keywords 46
Keyword Difficulties 47

Chapter 10 - Team Orders and Expert Teams 50
Team Orders 50
Expert Teams 51

Chapter 11 - Direct Orders 53
Why the Focus on DOs? 53
The Mechanics of DOs 54
A Note about Setting Client Rates 55

Chapter 12 - Your First Writing Jobs 56
First-Time Jitters 56
Focus on Open and Team Orders 56
Prepare Yourself to Attract Direct Orders 57
Deliver on Time 57
Drop Everything to Service a Revision Request 58
Communicating with Clients 58
Article Evaluations 58
What If Your Star Level Is Reduced? 59
Making Money Is the Name of the Game 60

Chapter 13 - Tips on Becoming a Profitable Copywriter 61
Familiarizing Yourself with Topics 61

    Speed is King for Per-Word Orders 61

    Avoid the Enemy of Done 62

    Take the Direct Approach 62

    Overcoming Writer's Block 63

    Never Stop Learning 64

Chapter 14 - Writing Resources 65

    Grammar References 65

    Writing Guides 65

    Tools 66

Chapter 15 - Textbroker Quirks 68

    HTML Translation 68

    Plain Text Formatting, Preview and Editing 71

    Order Vanishes After Submission 71

    Tallying Your Orders and Payments 72

Chapter 16 - Getting Help 73

    The FAQ, Forum and Email 73

    Textbroker University 73

    Opening a Client Account 74

Chapter 17 - Moving Beyond Textbroker 75

    Other Ways to Make Money Copywriting 75

Chapter 18 – Ready for the Journey 77

    My Path 77

    Starting Down Your Path Now 78

    Enjoy the Scenery and Tell Me How to Help 78

Table of Figures

Figure 1 My User Data Contact Information 18

Figure 2 My User Data Expertise Checkboxes 19

Figure 3 Your Author Home Page after Account Approval 20

Figure 4 Your User Profile Resume Section under the General Info Tab 21

Figure 5 The Bottom of the General Info Tab 22

Figure 6 Your Public Profile Abilities Tab 23

Figure 7 - Extremely Important Warning Seen Frequently on Textbroker's Site 29

Figure 8 Open Orders Search Panel for Filtering Pool Orders 34

Figure 9 – The OO Category Table Where You Start Your Selection of Open Orders 35

Figure 10 - Detailed Example of the Top Half of an Open Order 37

Figure 11 - Example of Too Much Detail That Spells Trouble (1,677 words total!) 41

Figure 12 - Example of Processing and Drop-Dead Deadlines 43

Figure 13 - Besides Team Invitations Open Casting Calls Offer Thousands of Opportunities 51

Figure 14 - Insert Word Rich Formatted Text via the TB Word Widget Popup 70

Figure 15 - How Word Rich Headings Come Out via TB's HTML Renderer 71

Setting Off on a New Journey 79

Preface

Who cannot use a little more money, especially in today's economy with stagnant wages while the cost of living continues to rise? Working two or even three jobs is sadly a new (albeit difficult) norm in the workaday world. Fortunately, a multitude of opportunities for much needed supplemental income exist thanks to the Internet.

For nearly any industry or market sector, the demand for skilled copywriters is expanding at an incredible pace. Long gone are the days when you could hit page one in Web searches by simply stuffing a page chock full of keywords or tags. Online information consumers demand real and relevant content, which is exactly what modern search engines strive to deliver. This means that a Web content producer desiring to place in the top of Google searches must have people who can write effective copy.

This book's mission is to convince you that you are one of those people and show you how to start writing great copy in the shortest time possible while guaranteeing you get paid for your work even as you are mastering copywriting skills.

The Textbroker content brokerage provides an excellent starting platform and a rapid path to higher earnings if you follow the guidance and tips this book offers you. Textbroker is not the only way to make money copywriting of course. That is why this book also prepares you to write copy on other content brokerages, freelance sites or via your own copywriting business.

The author claims no special expertise in writing. His background is engineering, not literature, although he has authored approximately half a million words on Textbroker, thousands of pages of technical documents, presentations and maintains four active blogs. He is proof that anyone with a desire to write can transform that desire into welcome extra income, which is why he wishes to pass on his experiential knowledge.

Chapter 1 - What You Will Learn from This Book

If you have considered creating a new source of income from copywriting, this book jump-starts your journey, starts you down the most effective path and assists you in becoming an efficient copywriter who regularly earns the highest rates. If you already have experience in copywriting, this book teaches you valuable tips to save yourself countless hours learning the ropes at Textbroker's site.

Here is an outline of the key topics in this book:

- What copywriting is, how much it pays and how to perform it most efficiently
- The attributes of successful copywriters
- Why Textbroker is an ideal platform for new copywriters
- Time-saving instructions on using Textbroker effectively
- How to increase your profits per article
- How to attract lucrative Direct Orders
- Tips for improving your writing
- Extensive lists of online resources that improve your efficiency
- Ideas for branching out from Textbroker to create your personal writing career

If you want to learn the ins and outs of copywriting, particularly the nuts and bolts of copywriting work on Textbroker, then this book has it all. You will quickly be on your way to tapping into a source of well-paying part-time or even full-time work.

Chapter 1 - What You Will Learn from This Book

Getting the Most from This Book in the Shortest Time Possible

Not everyone learns at the same pace or in the same manner. Each of us has an optimized channel for learning such as listening to lectures, reading material or absorbing information visually. For book learning, one very effective approach to quickly absorbing new material is what I call the skim-search-and-study method:

- Skim every chapter before diving into any single one. Avoid dwelling on any single part. Even though you may feel that you are not retaining anything in this manner, you are setting up your subconscious to rapidly absorb detailed information on subsequent passes.
- Search online for any topics, points or vocabulary that stood out for you during the skimming step. Again, do not linger long on what you find, as this tactic also prepares your mind for detailed learning later.
- Finally, using the Table of Contents or the Quick Start Guide, select chapters that are most relevant to you or simply read chapters fully after this one in sequential order.

As with any learning exercise, it pays big dividends to make sure you are rested, comfortable and in a place free from distractions. Good luck and welcome to Make Money Now Copywriting in Your Spare Time or *Earn While You Learn Copywriting on Textbroker*.

Chapter 2 – QUICK START GUIDE

You do not need to read this book from beginning to end. It has been organized in self-contained chapters that you can skip or mix in any order you like. The quick-start list below guides you toward specific topic areas that suit your needs or interests at any moment.

Chapter Overviews

- If you need an introduction to copywriting and why it could be the ideal work-at-home opportunity for you, then start with Chapter 3 and Chapter 4.
- Chapter 5 explains why Textbroker is such an ideal platform for beginning copywriters who want to understand the business, improve their writing and earn while they learn.
- If you want to open your Textbroker account and prepare to take orders, start with Chapter 6 and Chapter 7.
- Chapter 8 explains all the complexities of Textbroker Open Orders, how to select those that are easiest to work with and several potential order pitfalls.
- Chapter 9 teaches you how to overcome what is often a big stumbling block for any writer, article keywords, especially the awkward ones that must be "hammered" into place.
- Chapter 10 and Chapter 11 cover Team/Expert Orders and lucrative Direct Orders, respectively.

Chapter 2 – QUICK START GUIDE

- Chapter 12 and Chapter 13 are full of tips that are useful for new and experienced copywriters alike, such as how to avoid writer's block. These tips are critical to maximizing your profit potential.
- Chapter 14 contains many online writers' references and guides for checking and improving grammar and style, online tools such as capitalization and plagiarism checkers as well as other paying sites.
- Chapter 15 and Chapter 16 describe a few Textbroker interface quirks (e.g., HTML conversion) that may cause you confusion plus guides to the best online help resources to get you un-stuck.
- Chapter 17 discusses how to take your copywriting skills beyond Textbroker by applying them to other writing sites or starting your own writing business.
- Finally, Chapter 18 summarizes the typical journey to becoming a copywriter.

Chapter 3 - Introduction to Copywriting

What is Copywriting?

Copywriting is simply the writing of informative articles or descriptions that are used in promotional or advertising materials. You see it everywhere in blog posts, catalogs, flyers, white papers and the equivalent of printed or online infomercials. Although its purpose is to market or sell something either directly or indirectly, most copywriters on Textbroker are not writing explicit sales material, so you do not have to worry if you feel you are not cut out to be a salesman.

Why is that? Because on Textbroker, 99 percent of what you write is intended for online use such as a web page or a blog. Search engines, i.e. Google, attempt to rank search results based on the quality of information contained on the pages it indexes. Material that is overly "salesy" or outright spam gets severely punished in the rankings for the most part.

So, even though most of the material you write is at least indirectly pushing products or brand awareness, it does it subtly, which takes a lot of pressure off the writer. Frankly, writing highly effective sales copy is more art than science and requires a special skillset not needed for Textbroker copywriting.

Types of Copy You May Write

Here is a list of the types of copywriting you are likely to find on any given day on Textbroker:

Chapter 3 - Introduction to Copywriting

Product Descriptions

These are typically 50 +/- words in length, so they have to pack a lot of information in a short space. They simply describe a specific product's positive attributes and provide information such as size, weight, color choices or styles.

Product Reviews

These can describe a single product or a family of products and typically run between 200 and 1,000 words in length. Most clients want them to appear unbiased, so there is room for a few product disadvantages. They often consist of an overview, a callout of high-level features, technical specifications, a summary of buyer opinions and a conclusion with a rating. These are fairly easy to research and if you have several closely related products, they are fast to write. Sometimes, you will write a collection of product reviews as part of a lengthy buyer's guide.

Blog Articles

Sometimes, clients want one or two blog articles to fit within the theme of an existing blog. These articles usually run from 400 to 1,000 words long. If the company is small, the requirements may be loose, but big companies typically have a detailed specification to follow. The latter are a bit of a pain, but a terrific learning experience and could lead to Direct Orders.

Occasionally, a client hands you the task of writing all the posts on their blog on an ongoing basis. These can be extremely lucrative if they are posting a couple times a week or more. The first few require additional time, but as you get the hang of the subject area, you can write subsequent posts quickly.

Informative Articles

These are similar to blog posts, but are often longer, up to 2,000 words in length. These are used as info-collateral on web sites trying to claim authority in a subject area. For instance, a site that sells advertising to companies producing eco-friendly products might want articles discussing aspects of global warming or the use of renewable energy without naming specific products. They are often written in a semi-casual tone. These typically do not offer the frequency of blog articles, but if the client provides most of the research material for you they can be money-makers.

In-depth Articles

Truly in-depth articles are uncommon at the 4-star level, so you are unlikely to see such orders. Beware of them because they can require a significant amount of research effort and research is the number one killer of your hourly rate. These are upwards of 4,000 words, so make sure the deadline is adequate.

Case Studies

You might find Textbroker orders asking for a case study, but probably it is a case study in name only. True case studies require the most up-to-date information and involve interviewing experts in the topic field. These are rare, but when you see them the client should provide all the research material necessary to complete the writing, especially if it is an Open Order.

White Papers

White paper orders are typically about 1,500 to 2,500 words in length. They follow a specific style of outline provided for you or which you can look up online, so outlining the material is usually not necessary. They differ from case studies in that they are much more sales oriented. By the way, white papers are a lucrative sideline outside of Textbroker, though you have the additional burden of marketing your service.

Sales and Advertising Copy

This is copy for brochures, flyers, ads and even scripts for video commercials. You will rarely see these and as I noted they take a special set of skills to do right, so it is best to pass them up on Textbroker if you are new to copywriting.

Chapter 4 - The Benefits of Copywriting as a Job/Career

Do You Like to Write?

If you like writing at all – even just a letter home - and savor the idea of making money on your own at your own pace, then copywriting on Textbroker can be a great job. It has a number of general benefits:

- You get to write and feel appreciation for your efforts via monetary compensation
- You can take on as little or as much of it as you like
- You can choose the type of articles you like to write the most
- You can stretch your writing skills by finding article assignments a bit away from your knowledge
- You choose the hours in any given day during which to write
- You choose where to write, whether it be in your home an office or the local coffee shop

How You Make Money Copywriting

Copywriters can earn a salary, work by the piece or get paid by the word.

Earning a salary means the copywriter works for one company. Usually they work only on copy for that company's products or marketing collateral, but it is possible that the product is copy that is hired out to other companies.

For sites such as Textbroker, the pay is strictly by the word (although client tips are possible). Many clients prefer this arrangement, of course,

Chapter 4 - The Benefits of Copywriting as a Job/Career

because their costs are predictable and the price per word provides a rough gauge of the quality of work to expect.

Pricing copy by the piece is often the practice of the most experienced and skilled copywriters. They produce complete articles, white papers, and so on that are ready to print, including images, without further editing or formatting.

By-the-piece writers are more often than not freelancers that run their own business, do their own marketing and handle all the payments and expenses directly. This area can be the most lucrative at all, but it is not for the faint of heart and not for people unwilling to work at it full-time especially during the first few years.

What You Need to be Successful at Copywriting

Enjoyment of Writing

The number one contributor to success for a copywriter is simply the enjoyment of writing being present. Ninety percent of the time, people who like to write have a knack for it. They've received compliments on their writing from friends, family, a teacher, a colleague or a boss. Even if you like to write but consider that your writing is poor, you still have the first piece of the puzzle within your grasp. Writing naturally becomes more enjoyable the more you do it and the more you learn about it.

Grammar

Grammar is simply rules and they can be memorized through study and practice. You actually only need to learn a fraction of English grammar rules to be successful at copywriting. Most of the arcane, rarely-used rules you will never encounter when writing on Textbroker. Textbroker supplies plenty of help in avoiding the most common grammar mistakes. Their occasional reviews of your articles will correct your bad habits quickly.

Structure

Outlining

Well-structured writing is a skill easily learned. The first step is to learn about outlining. Outlining is simply a quick way to set forth the flow of your article at a high level. If you can refine the outline down to sections that only require 100-200 words each to fill out, you will find that the articles practically write themselves.

Logical Argument

Another aspect to structure involves setting forth your article's "argument" from the introduction to the conclusion. This is a critical factor in addition to grammar and spelling that separates 2-star, 3-star and 4-star writers.

Avoiding Fluff

A third component of good structure is the avoidance of filler text or "fluff" that adds little or nothing to the message you are trying to impart to the reader. Once you have written for a while, filler will stand out to you in stark contrast to the surrounding text or meaning within your articles.

You can read plenty of material online such as this guide from Dartmouth University on how to organize a paper [https://writing-speech.dartmouth.edu/learning/materials-first-year-writers/considering-structure-and-organization] to help you improve your structure. 6 Tips for Avoiding Filler and Fluffy Writing in Your Content [http://www.contentcustoms.com/blog/6-tips-avoiding-filler-fluffy-writing-content] is an excellent blog post to call out your fluff and eliminate it.

Patience and Determination

You will not make top money at first on Textbroker. You need to put in the time in the Open Order pool, take their Textbroker University courses and study off-site on a regular basis. It will be months or even a year (as in my case) before you get a steady stream of Direct Orders and can start upping your rates. How fast you reach higher rates is directly proportional to how much effort you put in.

Chapter 5 - Why Write on Textbroker?

Even though Textbroker is still my primary brokerage source for online writing jobs, there are others, such as iWriter or WriterAccess that connect clients and authors. I've simply found that Textbroker offers all that I need and in a fairly straightforward manner. In my opinion, it's the best of the bunch in terms of getting your first paid articles under your belt in an environment conducive to quickly learning how to write copy.

Here are the principal benefits that I find compelling about Textbroker:

Bare Minimum of Marketing Required

You are relieved of nearly all the tedium of marketing yourself and your writing. This is a biggie, since freelancers can easily spend half their time finding clients, especially when they are starting out. The bulk of your marketing, aimed at getting Direct Orders, is an online portfolio of a few articles or snippets of articles that display your expertise. These can be deferred while to start taking Open Orders. The only other "marketing" required is to promptly answer queries from potential clients via the Textbroker messaging system.

Superb Learning Platform

From Day One on Textbroker, you have access to their online grammar courses, the writer's forum and 24/7 email access to author support experts. An initial writing sample will be evaluated to determine your "star rating," which will be 2, 3 or 4 stars (5 stars requires additional work). Textbroker will continue to evaluate your work by sampling not

Chapter 5 - Why Write on Textbroker?

by looking at every article. These evaluations should be viewed as personalized learning opportunities rather than seeing them as criticism.

Another learning aspect to Textbroker is that you are exposed to an enormous variety of topic areas. Currently, as I write this, the Open Orders page has 40 topic areas from Arts and Crafts to Home and Family to Science and thousands of article orders within those categories.

Naturally, you will tend to gravitate toward topics in which you already have knowledge, which is my recommended way to begin. In order to earn more, however, you will need to branch out into other topic areas, some of which may be on the border of your comfort zone. Do not worry, as I am going to help you with that. You will be surprised how easy it is to expand your writing repertoire by becoming an expert in almost any copywriting topic.

Increasing Flow of Work

We will cover different order types in more detail later, but for now remember there are basically three types of writing orders: Open Orders, Team Orders and Direct Orders. Any author can pick up an Open Order if it is rated equal to or less than their current star rating. You also receive invites to writing teams that focus on a particular topic, which you can take or leave without penalty. These typically pay more than Open Orders.

In short, there are a wide variety of orders and over the years I have witnessed a marked increase in the number of topic categories and the sheer number of orders overall.

Guaranteed Payment without a Middle Man

One of the few requirements you must meet to write on Textbroker is to have a PayPal account. There is no alternative method of payment.

The good news here is that unlike other pay-to-write sites, Textbroker picks up any commission charged by PayPal, so you get exactly the amount in your account as what you saw on the order. If the order is for 500-600 words at 3 cents a word and you wrote 550 words, you will receive $16.50 for that article in your PayPal account.

Chapter 5 - Why Write on Textbroker?

Textbroker pays weekly. As long as you have $10 or more in your account, you can request a payout. You must request the payout no later than midnight on Thursday to receive it Friday.

Textbroker Drawbacks

Naturally, no copywriting broker is perfect. The drawbacks to Textbroker are actually shared by most brokers.

Low Pay to Start

Pay is low when you are first starting out, which is why I show you how to raise your star rating and get onto Direct Orders as quickly as possible. The best attitude to take during this period is to realize you are still in the learning phase, and think about how few other educational situations pay you as you learn.

Order Droughts

Orders, especially Open Orders, do dry up occasionally. January, for instance, is typically a slow month for orders as companies are re-evaluating their copywriting efforts for the coming year (although I've been swamped with orders in January at times). The way to deal with these periods of low orders is to join as many teams as you can, work on your writer's profile, study up on your grammar weak spots, open an account on another broker's site or polish your freelancing plan.

The Walled Garden

Textbroker, like other copywriting portals, tries to facilitate their authors' efforts, but the honest truth is that their bread and butter comes from the clients. Thus, they protect the identity of their clients fiercely in various ways, one of which is to limit all communication between authors and clients to their on-site messaging system.

Full names are not allowed for either clients or authors. Any possibly identifying information in personal messages between clients and authors is scrutinized and messages with such information are blocked. Their Terms of Service for both clients and authors specify strict and punitive steps should individuals from the two camps collaborate on writing jobs outside of Textbroker. See more about this topic in Chapter 7.

Chapter 5 - Why Write on Textbroker?

Limited Ability to Market Yourself

I wrote earlier that one of the advantages of using Textbroker is that your marketing effort as a freelancer is minimal. That is actually a two-edged sword. Your Textbroker author profile is the primary marketing tool you possess, but it is limited. Your writing samples are in plain text for one thing. Outreach is from clients to authors, never the other way around. They can search for keywords, which helps if you included relevant ones in your profile. When clients do contact you, this does provide an additional opportunity to market your skills however.

Basic UI on the Writers Portal

When you login to Textbroker, you enter a username and password. The author/client check boxes determine which side of the portal you see. I encourage you to open a client account in addition to your author account so you can see what life is like on the other side. This will provide you with some empathy for clients, plus open your eyes as to the sparseness of the user interface on the author side.

Clients receiving priority is as it should be. Personally, however, I do wish more attention was paid to a number of "glitches" in the author-side interface that have persisted for the several years I have written on Textbroker. I'll alert you to these in Chapter 15 so you don't waste time when you encounter one of these quirks.

Is Textbroker's Commission Too High?

Textbroker adds 35% to what you get paid for an article, which results in a final price to the client. Most clients do not realize what this commission is, which you will find out if you ever mention your author rate in a message with a client. Thus, if my rate for a particular article is, say, 3 cents a word, the client actually pays 4.05 cents per word.

Every *author* on Textbroker knows about this commission and some complain that it is too bit a cut (although it is in line with other brokerages). My viewpoint is to consider what I would have to spend in terms of both time and money to find clients myself, which leaves me thinking their cut is fair.

Chapter 5 - Why Write on Textbroker?

Frankly, I hate marketing my talents. It is my least favorite aspect to writing probably because I'm poor at it. As long as Textbroker supplies me with a solid supply of work and continues to grant me a path to greater earnings and does not mess with my own rate, I do not bother myself with what they charge clients.

Chapter 6 - Getting Started on Textbroker

Are you ready to get started writing on Textbroker? Then this is the chapter that tells you how to do that in a hurry.

I'll cover all the details of getting your account started, where and how to start looking for work in the most efficient manner including what to avoid and how to get your work done quickly with high quality.

Account Setup

Important Qualifications

Besides the desire to write, you need three basic qualifications to open a Textbroker author account:

1. You must be a U.S. Citizen or Permanent Resident of the U.S. and able to supply a W-9 form
2. You must be 18 years of age or older
3. You must have a PayPal account, which implies that you also have an email address

If you do not meet these qualifications, there is still much to learn from this book about copywriting that will serve you well on other copywriting brokerage or freelance site such as vWriter or iWriter. It is slightly less useful with regard to freelance sites, such as UpWork, where half your time will be spent chasing clients versus actually writing.

Note that you are not required to be a native English speaker or writer, as long as you can meet the writing mechanics, grammar and spelling standards for the star level at which you are rated.

Other Requirements

Microsoft Word

While not necessary to open your TB account, to work on the site you need a recent version of Microsoft Word. This requirement is not strictly necessary if you were only submitting plain text, but whether your articles are in plain text or HTML is up to the client not you. HTML-formatted articles are created in Word using normal heading and other formatting and then pasted via a specialized Word widget that turns those headings and so forth into HTML. I've tried it with a couple of other editors and it simply did not work.

AP Style

Another strict requirement is that your writing must adhere to the Associated Press Style Guide, called AP Style for short. There are several style guides that writers use such as Chicago Manual of Style or MLA Style, but TB's is AP Style, nothing else.

The guide is lengthy and meticulously detailed. Although it is updated each year, you could easily get by with an older version, since the vast majority of your writing is unlikely to touch even 20% of it. For those of you familiar with AP Style, you may have already noticed that I'm not following it in this book, which allows me a bit more stylistic freedom (such as the use of parentheses, which AP Style abhors).

Walk-Through of Application Steps

Remember that when you start the account setup process to click on Author and not Client (I actually recommend elsewhere that you also open a Client account, but I digress ...).

As part of the application process, you select the Account tab and the My User Data menu item. This brings you to a page named Change User Data, which contains your basic contact information, a checkbox selection of your topic expertise and PayPal address. You can see examples of contact info and expertise choices in Figures 1 and 2.

Chapter 6 - Getting Started on Textbroker

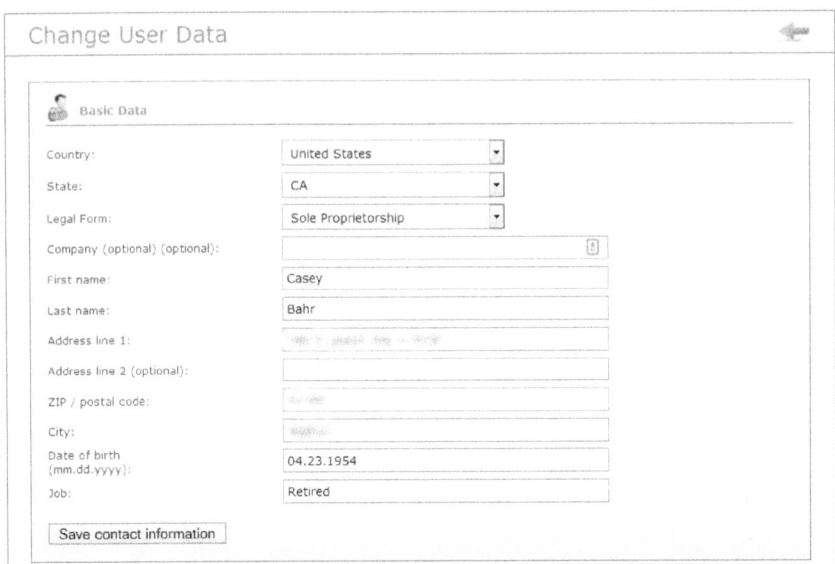

Figure 1 My User Data Contact Information

The list of countries in your basic data is supposedly where you reside, but remember that you must be a U.S. citizen or U.S. resident with a work permit to use Textbroker as an author. Thus, I took this pull-down menu to be the country where I am a citizen (the U.S.), even though I reside in Costa Rica. I must, however, submit a U.S. mailing address, which I have.

The Legal Form pull-down refers to your U.S. tax entity status. Most authors are work-at-home freelancers like me, in which case sole proprietorship is the correct choice. However, select whatever is accurate for your situation. It is out of the scope of this book and my expertise to recommend options for your specific situation.

The remainder of the top section of the form is self-explanatory.

Near the bottom of the application page are a matrix of checkboxes for indicating your personal areas of expertise as seen in Figure 2. You have to choose at least two boxes. Your choices have no effect on whether your application will be approved or not and it is easy to modify these selections after approval, so just pick a couple that you know something about and move to the bottom of the page.

Chapter 6 - Getting Started on Textbroker

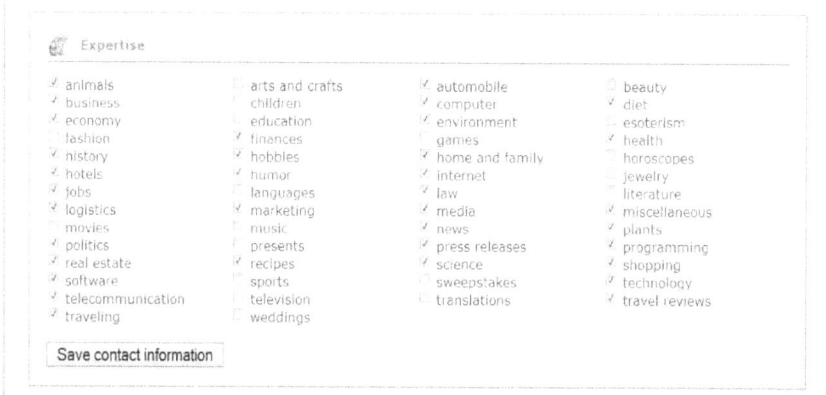

Figure 2 My User Data Expertise Checkboxes

Personally, I interpret the word "expertise" loosely in this context. I'd hesitate to call myself an "expert" in *all* the areas I have checked off in Figure 2. Instead, I chose these topic areas from the standpoint that I know *something* about these subjects and I am confident that I could spin up on them for a specific article in a relatively short time.

After hundreds of articles written as a copywriter, I have learned to wear a lot of topical hats and so will you. I would never have checked nearly so many topic areas when I first started at Textbroker, but over time I've gained confidence that I could write excellent copy for any of those checked off.

Below these sections is a login change form and a line to enter your PayPal address.

The final task in account setup is to indicate that you have read their privacy policy and the terms of conditions for being an author on Textbroker. If you do not actually read the dozens of pages of legalese contained in those documents, I will neither blame you nor tell anyone you didn't. I'm actually going to defer discussing the Textbroker Terms of Service until Chapter 7, since it deserves detailed attention to a couple of critical points and I do not want to interrupt the account setup description with that. However, be very sure that you read Chapter 7.

Chapter 6 - Getting Started on Textbroker

Your Textbroker Profile

Once you have set up your account and it is approved, your next login takes you to your summary page similar to Figure 3.

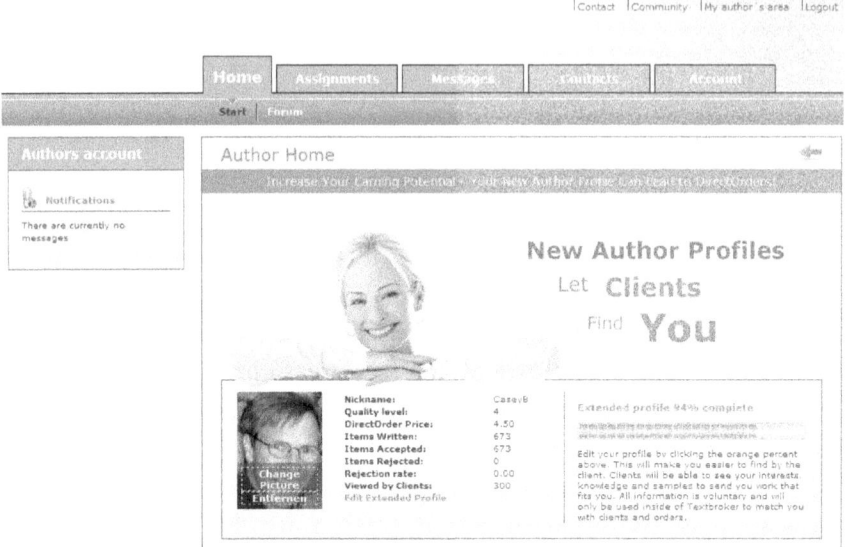

Figure 3 Your Author Home Page after Account Approval

From there go to your Account tab and visit your profile page, which you will find under menu item Public Profile. Filling out key items there is extremely important if you want to attract Direct Orders or even Team Orders. Start with an attractive headshot for your photo.

In the resume section, summarize your hobbies, interests, educational background (include certifications), plus your life or work experience to date. Use my profile resume in Figure 4 as an example.

Chapter 6 - Getting Started on Textbroker

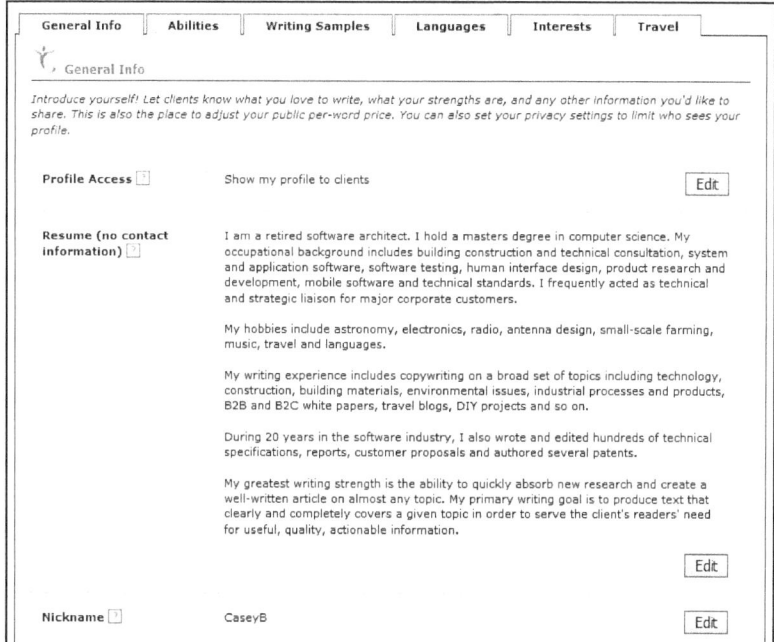

Figure 4 Your User Profile Resume Section under the General Info Tab

Even though this section is labeled "resume," my advice is to keep it brief, do not date anything and break it up into several short paragraphs. Too much detail here may result in potential clients missing the trees for the forest. Your goal is to simply make a quick, agreeable impression. You can expand on your abilities, interests, languages and travel experience in the other tabs named for those areas.

In case my resume is difficult to read in the figure, here it is in text:

Here it is in text:

"I am a retired software architect. I hold a master's degree in computer science. My occupational background includes building construction and technical consultation, system and application software, software testing, human interface design, product research and development, mobile software and technical standards. I frequently acted as technical and strategic liaison for major corporate customers.

My hobbies include astronomy, electronics, radio, antenna design, small-scale farming, music, travel and languages.

Chapter 6 - Getting Started on Textbroker

My writing experience includes copywriting on a broad set of topics including technology, construction, building materials, environmental issues, industrial processes and products, B2B and B2C white papers, travel blogs, DIY projects and so on.

During 20 years in the software industry, I also wrote and edited hundreds of technical specifications, reports, customer proposals and authored several patents.

My greatest writing strength is the ability to quickly absorb new research and create a well-written article on almost any topic. My primary writing goal is to produce text that clearly and completely covers a given topic in order to serve the client's readers' need for useful, quality, actionable information."

Figure 5 shows the remainder of the General Info tab information you can edit, which includes the Nickname shown to clients, your Direct Order price, your weekly writing capacity and an Away Message.

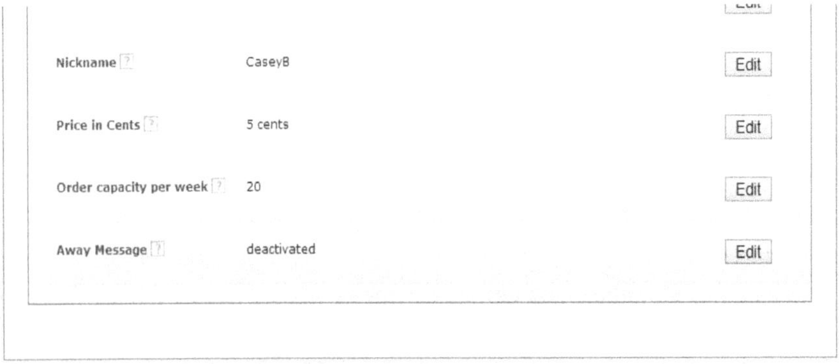

Figure 5 The Bottom of the General Info Tab

Your Nickname can be almost anything you want but must not reveal information that would permit a client to find you outside of Textbroker (such as your last name).

The Price in Cents is your Direct Order price per word. Whenever you change this price it is temporarily grayed out until Textbroker approves it although I'm not sure what there is to approve since it's up to you.

Order capacity per week is based on 500 word articles. I average about 500 words per hour (with a large variance) and do not want to obligate

Chapter 6 - Getting Started on Textbroker

myself to more than 20 hours per week, which is how I arrived at 20 articles per week.

The Away Message will be shown to clients visiting your profile if you turn it on. Use that when on vacation or otherwise absent for a few to several days. Filling this in is completely optional.

Abilities Tab

The Abilities Tab (mistakenly labeled General Info), seen in Figure 6, summarizes your educational and occupational background including the types of work you do. It also is a place to list the types of writing jobs you prefer. So, in a way it is an extension of your brief resume summary. Be sure to fill out this tab and remember you can always come back and tweak it at any time.

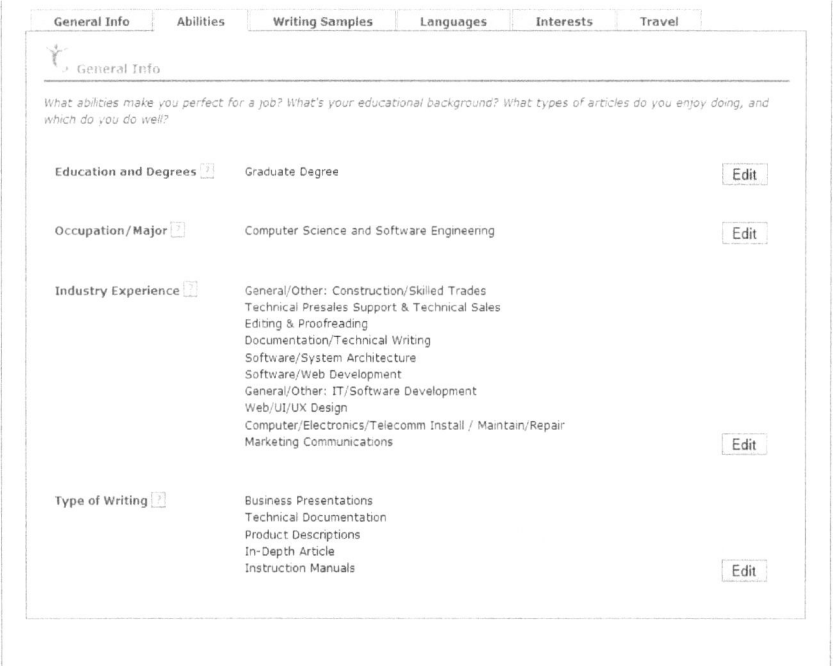

Figure 6 Your Public Profile Abilities Tab

Writing Samples

I would say this tab is of equal or more importance than your resume summary. Your samples have terrific power to sway clients your way. These are your sharpest marketing tool.

Chapter 6 - Getting Started on Textbroker

Do not worry if you lack existing samples at the present moment, however, because it is OK to use your articles from Textbroker, of which you will have a good selection very shortly. By the way, the message at the top of the tab says the samples are to be examples of writing you have not sold, but Textbroker staff said it is fine to use TB articles I've written.

Be sure these samples are as polished as possible and represent your best writing. Aspects of good Web content writing are discussed throughout this book. However, I recommend that you refer to the many writer's resources you can find online, many of which are listed in the Resources chapter, Chapter 14, later in this book to provide additional ideas about how to improve these samples over time.

You can submit up to three writing samples in your profile. There is no figure provided here because this tab is very straightforward. You simply indicate the type of writing, the title and the actual sample.

The question mark popup by "Writing Sample" informs you that the maximum word count per sample is 200 words, but all my samples are far longer than that.

By the way, even though my samples are entire articles, I'm ambivalent about using samples this long. My theory is that these extended samples not only show my writing style but my ability to construct longer articles with a convincing argument flow. I am quite sure that even 200 word snippets, however, would be quite effective if well-written.

Other Profile Tabs

Personally, I am not sure how valuable it is to list your interests, the countries you have visited (unless your writing specialty will be travel articles of course!) nor the languages you speak. Especially with regard to the latter, you are going to be writing primarily in U.S. English although occasionally there are UK English articles requested. I'm not confident that my British is up to the task of writing those correctly, so I always skip those. I'd say the last three tabs are optional or at least do not require the concentrated attention that the first three tabs do.

A Complete Profile Is Easier for Clients to Find

A complete profile is not only to impress drive-by visitors. Textbroker clients are able to search for authors based on keywords related to experience, topics, interests and education level. Thus, making sure your profile is thorough ensures that clients can find you in the first place.

The Bottom Line with Your Profile

Whether you are a novice or advanced in copywriting, do not let creating a super-duper profile put you off or slow you down. You can always improve it later at any time.

As you gain more experience writing articles, you will develop a better sense of what clients are looking for plus you will have a better selection of articles from which you can extract writing samples. I have completely changed my writing samples three times over the course of a few years of TB writing, for instance.

Even though your profile holds a prominent position in your effort to draw Direct Orders, it is far more important to simply write and write frequently. When you produce articles, you are essentially in direct contact with potential DO clients.

If they are impressed with your writing, they will check your profile for confirmation of your skills. This is especially true of clients who have been using Textbroker for a long time. Those clients who check your profile first before seeing an article you wrote for them are probably newer to TB.

Chapter 7 – Textbroker Terms of Service (Do Not Skip!)

Accepting the Textbroker Terms of Service

At some point, you are asked to accept Textbroker's Terms of Service and, perhaps like every other lengthy legal document for which it seems you have no choice but to agree, you are tempted just to click the box and move on without reading it. That's cool, I do the same thing 99 percent of the time. However, I urge you to take the time to read the next few pages concerning the most critical parts of the TOS that you must keep in mind while working with Textbroker.

Textbroker's Apprehension

Textbroker has one big fear, which leads to them separating clients and authors from one another as is practically feasible. If clients and author actually knew how to contact each other directly, they might do so in large numbers in order to avoid Textbroker's commission (and perhaps to avoid the rather awkward user interface through which they are forced to communicate). This has led them to spend a good deal of resources in terms of site development and processes designed to maintain a barrier of anonymity between writers and clients.

The TB Walled Garden

The "walled garden" design of Textbroker's site is perfectly understandable with regard to TB's business model. They are not an

Chapter 7 – Textbroker Terms of Service (Do Not Skip!)

introduction service, and they want to preserve their primary assets, which include both authors and clients.

You feel the effects of this segregation every time you visit the TB site. It starts with your own author profile, which prohibits that you include any personally identifiable information including your user name. You will also feel it during author-client communications via their messaging system. Each message is monitored by TB staff to make sure there is no mention of full names, locations or links that could give clues to the identity of either the author or client.

It's not a perfect system. With a little elbow grease and prodigious use of Google Search, it is possible to track down who is on the other end of the client-author relationship, especially for authors. Textbroker knows this, so they recently revised their TOS to wield a big stick in case authors and clients are tempted to work directly.

Memorize This Part of Textbroker's TOS (OK, Just Memorize My Summary)

The short story of that revision without the legalese is that if they discover that a TB author and a TB client are working together outside their walled garden, they will punish both of you. It starts with an automatic $500 fine for both parties plus a 5 cents/word penalty on whatever they think you wrote. You are also likely to be banned from Textbroker permanently. These conditions apply even after you leave Textbroker for a period of two years.

There was vigorous discussion in the TB author forum when the revised TOS came out especially with regard to this section. The bottom line is that it is questionable how Textbroker would actually enforce these provisions (unless you foolishly had $500 in your TB account at the time of discovery), but who wants to be the first author to find out? Even if innocent, TB authors tend to be part-timers, so having to defend themselves against a claim from Textbroker via a lawyer would likely be a significant economic hit.

Chapter 7 – Textbroker Terms of Service (Do Not Skip!)

Avoiding the Temptation of Direct Contact

Frankly, there are a number of inconvenient aspects and downright bugs in Textbroker's authors interface that at times I find frustrating. That and the idea that I could be picking up that extra 35% if I were working for a client directly presents a temptation to cheat.

On the other hand, TB is supplying me significant benefits that I would not have if I was dealing directly with clients. For one thing, I'm practically guaranteed rapid payment for my work as the client has to put up the money before they make an order. Also, TB guides the article specification process on the client side, which saves me a lot of time in trying to figure out exactly what the client wants.

Besides, clients come and go. The person ordering articles may change jobs or find a writer they like better or simply be moved to another assignment that does not require writing services.

If I were strictly a freelancer, I would have to crank up my marketing efforts again to replace a lost client. As long as I'm in Textbroker, I can simply turn to the open pool or find Team Orders to keep my work queue full and attract new Direct Order clients. I can also easily ignore or even blacklist clients that become troublesome, which is not so simple if you have direct contact and want to avoid a bad review of your services.

I hope you now clearly understand the motivations behind Textbroker's way of doing business and why it is, overall, in your best interests to stay within the limits of the client-author relationship as they proscribe it. Naturally, nothing is stopping you from working on your own, through other brokers or freelance sites for other clients, which, by the way, is a natural progression as your content writing skills expand over time.

Chapter 7 – Textbroker Terms of Service (Do Not Skip!)

One More Big (Actually Huge!) No-No: Plagiarism

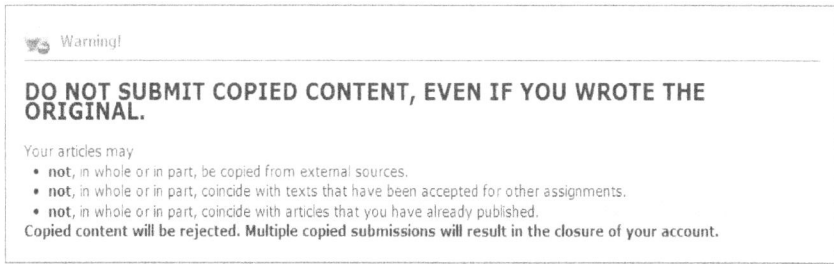

Figure 7 - Extremely Important Warning Seen Frequently on Textbroker's Site

Clients have a 100% expectation that the content provided by Textbroker writers is original, i.e. not copied from someone else's work. In Western music because of its relatively limited range of elements and range of expression, unintentional plagiarism (e.g., Led Zeppelin's *Stairway to Heaven* lawsuit) sometimes occurs. In the world of writing, accidentally writing a 100 words in exactly the same way as someone else wrote them is extremely unlikely.

Without being overly detailed and pedantic about the definition of plagiarism, I assume the reader has a conscience and will know themselves when they have crossed this line by, say, cutting and pasting in a paragraph or even a phrase verbatim from someone else's work, which also includes your own published work. The guilt-buzzer built into your brain will surely be activated.

Fortunately, "original" in this case is not being used in the sense that the ideas within your article are completely your own. No one in their right mind has such high expectations of writers they pay by the word. Thus, it is perfectly all-right to read another article that relates to the one you are writing and paraphrase or rework the content. Just do the paraphrasing very thoroughly. Do not simply replace a few words in a sentence as that will still leave you in a gray zone.

I can always think of at least half a dozen ways right off the bat to say what has been said before in a unique manner using a variety of phrases, tone, flow, examples and even differing argument lines. Even for short articles I may peruse 10 or more articles that are topic-related, skim them and pull off key ideas I want to include in my article. After re-writing and re-organizing the content you would never be able to pinpoint the sources.

My brief description of how I transpose research into my writing probably sounds more complex and difficult than it actually is. Research and rework typically takes about 20-25% of the total writing time. So, there is no reason, not even time-saving, to try and copy content once you get the hang of finding information quickly and getting your outline, ideas and paragraphs onto virtual paper rapidly.

How Will They Know?

Believe me, there are plenty of online tools available to track down plagiarism in a hurry and with TB's corporate budget they can afford the best tools. Their reputation depends on providing original content, so they focus on this area just about as hard as they do maintaining the client-writer separation wall.

Now, I have to confess that TB caught copied content in one of my articles. One sentence to be exact. It was not intentional on my part but the result of a bad habit and poor proofreading. My style is to cut-and-paste snippets from other articles and insert them in my draft. At one time, I pasted this stuff in using the same Normal formatting as my own writing. This time it was a snippet from one of my past articles on the same topic.

Since it was my own wording, on the final edit I missed it but they caught it almost immediately. Since then, of course, if I do the cut-n-paste technique I always change the snippet to a bright red color.

I think what I did was probably the least egregious form of copying that TB sees, but beware that they will only let a few plagiarisms go by before they will cancel your account. That is a high price to pay indeed for saving a few minutes of time.

If you are a bit paranoid about accidentally plagiarizing, utilize one or more of the free online plagiarism tools referenced in the Writers Resources chapter near the end of the book.

Chapter 8 – Deciphering TB Orders

Understanding writing orders is key to your success, so I go into a lot of detail in this chapter. It's a long one, so settle back and enjoy the ride.

Order Types

There are four types of writing orders that you will see. I briefly list these below with full descriptions in this and subsequent chapters:

- **Open Orders** – Also known as "the pool," these are orders available to any writer within the limits of their star rating. They pay the lowest rates.
- **Team Orders** – These are orders available to a smaller subset of writers. Sometimes you are solicited to join, but there are "open" teams to which you can apply too. Rates vary widely from about 10 to 30 percent more than Open Orders up to double or triple the Open Order rates.
- **Expert Teams** – These are similar to Team Orders but are more specific in the requirements they impose on writers. Typically, they require deeper technical expertise and thus pay higher rates than generic Team Orders.
- **Direct Orders** – Textbroker clients use Direct Orders to solicit a specific author because they were impressed either by your Open Order work or by the writing samples in your profile and your listed areas of expertise. You set the rates for Direct Orders. I'll explain later why, in TB slang, "DOs" are where you want to be in your TB career.

Chapter 8 – Deciphering TB Orders

Writer Star Levels Explained

Writer star levels range from two to five. There is no such thing as a one star TB writer. I don't know why. Initially, when you start your account you submit a short writing sample on one of a few topics of their choice (e.g., the attractions of the town you live in). Their evaluation of this sample determines your initial star rating of two, three or four stars.

A rating of five stars requires 100 percent perfect grammar, spelling and article structure. It also requires that you pass a stringent proofreading test and perform actual proofreading for a period of time. I readily admit that I am not qualified to be a five star writer (yet) and I'm convinced that it is not necessary to strive for that either. Four stars is what you should set your sights on. You will make good money and get better assignments. Obtaining that level is not as difficult as you might think.

Once you have your star rating, you are good to go as far as snatching Open Orders, Team Orders and Direct Orders, all of which are explained in detail shortly.

Open Orders

Since you are going to be starting with Open Orders, the remainder of this chapter deals specifically with those followed by separate chapters for Team and Direct Orders. All order types use the same order form, so there is an overlap of information among them.

Open Orders or "pool orders" as TB veterans call them are where everyone starts including five star writers. The Open Order page presents you with a matrix of writing orders ready for the taking. Down the left hand side will be a large number of article categories such as Travel, Law, Business, Sports, Health and so on. Across the page are four columns, one for each star rating from two to five. Each row displays the count for each star level of articles looking for writers in that particular category.

Open Order Rates

You are free to pick up any article that is in your star rating or below. Thus, a 4-star writer always has the biggest pool of Open Orders available to them whereas the 2-star writer can only select from the 2-star

Chapter 8 – Deciphering TB Orders

column. Five star writers get two cents per word for pool orders. Four star writers receive 1.4 cents per word while 3-star writers get one cent per word and 2-star writers receive 0.7 cents per word.

Obviously, no one is getting rich at these rates, but do not fret about that because the game plan is to dwell as short a time as possible in the pool. Furthermore, if you are a copywriting novice, consider these rates to be gravy because you will be getting paid to learn how to be a better copywriter who can quickly raise your star rating or move up to other, more lucrative, order types.

Choosing an Open Order

When clicking on an article count, a new page opens up that displays all the Open Orders for that category. All you will have to go on when choosing one to examine more closely at this point is a title and word count. When you click on a title, a new page opens up displaying all the details of the order.

When you first display an order, you may feel overwhelmed by all the information it contains. You are going to feel a lot less overwhelmed, however, because we shortly discuss the "anatomy" of an Open Order so you can focus on the most important parameters and quickly decide if this order is a good one for you.

Not only does this improve your efficiency (and thus your hourly rate), but it is also necessary as there is a 10-minute limit for examination of a single order, the intricacies of which will be discussed shortly.

Open Order Ebb and Flow

After writing for Textbroker out of the pool for a month or two, you will notice that the amount of orders vary from week to week or month to month. There will be times, especially in January, where it virtually dries up and the only orders available are stinkers that no one else wanted to take (you shouldn't either because there are probably good reasons, which I'll cover later, why they are stinkers). When the pool is dry like that, it is an excellent time to dig into Team Orders or catch up on those grammar tutorials you've been putting off.

Chapter 8 – Deciphering TB Orders

Open Order Visual Anatomy

With the help of screenshots, let's see what is in a typical Open Order. We'll start with the Open Order category page, which is where you start any Open Order search.

Open Order Top Level Page

At the top of the OO Category page is a search panel (see Figure 8) to help narrow your search. Honestly, I have never tweaked this beyond the default settings shown below, but I can see where keyword search, Client ID and the Category selector could be useful.

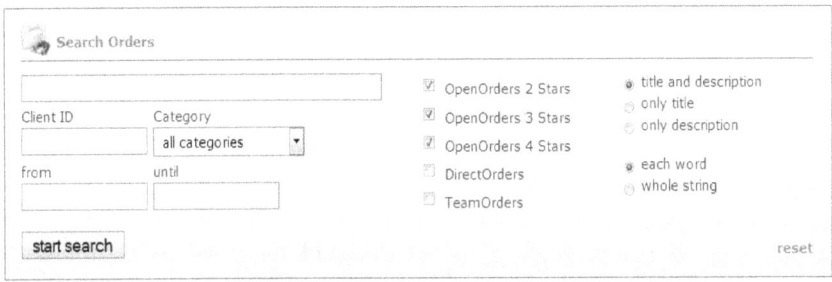

Figure 8 Open Orders Search Panel for Filtering Pool Orders

Chapter 8 – Deciphering TB Orders

Category					
automobile	213	0	132	81	0
beauty	19	0	12	7	0
business	216	0	159	56	1
computer	11	0	1	9	1
education	19	0	1	18	0
environment	4	0	4	0	0
fashion	4	0	0	3	1
finances	18	0	3	15	0
games	41	0	0	41	0
health	207	0	10	195	2
hobbies	9	0	0	9	0
home and family	19	0	0	19	0
hotels	1	0	0	0	1
humor	1	0	0	1	0
internet	14	0	0	14	0
jewelry	1	0	0	1	0
jobs	180	0	3	177	0
law	24	0	0	24	0
logistics	3	0	0	3	0
marketing	79	0	0	79	0
miscellaneous	824	0	759	63	2
music	7	0	0	7	0
news	4	0	0	4	0
press releases	3	0	0	2	1
programming	25	0	0	25	0
real estate	11	0	6	5	0
shopping	13	0	0	13	0
software	8	0	0	6	2
sports	7	0	0	7	0
sweepstakes	1	0	0	1	0
technology	70	0	1	68	1
telecommunication	1	0	0	1	0
translations	29	0	29	0	0
traveling	3	0	2	1	0
weddings	3	0	3	0	0

Figure 9 – The OO Category Table Where You Start Your Selection of Open Orders

As you can see in Figure 9, there are 35 topic categories displayed down the left side. Depending on their current order batches, more or less categories may be displayed.

The "stars" columns represent how many Open Orders are available in each category for each star level.

Note that even though there is no check box for 5-star orders in the search box, the 5-star column is displayed. It does not always display zero jobs available, but far more often than not the jobs there will be sparse with category counts in single digits.

Chapter 8 – Deciphering TB Orders

Keep an Eye on this Table

It is interesting, even if you are not looking specifically for Open Orders, to glance at this table from time to time. The numbers in aggregate and for particular categories can vary a great deal. In fact, the snapshot of Open Orders above in Figure 9 is atypical in that usually there are more (up to 5 times) 4-star orders than 3-star orders. However, you can see that 4-star orders cover far more categories. Note also that there are few 5-star orders, which is typical and which is one reason I feel that the 4-star level is the sweet spot.

In any case, glancing at this table occasionally provides you with a rough estimate for Web content demand in general. For example, you'll often see hundreds or thousands of Open Orders for a single category especially during the U.S. holiday season. Once you become a Direct Order writer, however, these kinds of fluctuations are unlikely to affect you noticeably.

Open Order Details

To look at specific orders, you click on the orange-ish numbers in the Category matrix. If you click on a number in the Total column, you will see all orders for all the star levels you chose in the search panel for that particular category. If you click on a number in a stars column, you get only those orders for that specific category at that star level.

For example, if you were to click on the Business category for 3-star writers, a paginated list of 159 orders is displayed, each of which show a title, star level, number of days for completion once you accept, the word count range and the price range you will be paid.

In the example below in Figure 10, I have clicked on an order in the Business category. For legibility, only the top half of the order form is shown in Figure 10. Certain information is blurred to protect client privacy.

Chapter 8 – Deciphering TB Orders

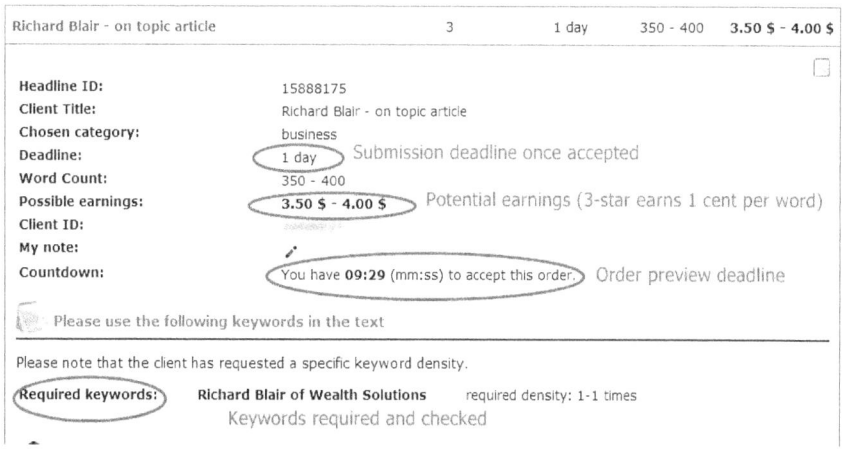

Figure 10 - Detailed Example of the Top Half of an Open Order

I purposely blurred some of the information in the order example in Figure 10 to obscure the client's identity although this order is rather old by the time you're seeing it. Here are explanations of the most important fields:

- **Client Title** – Unless the directions at the bottom of the order say otherwise, use the supplied title verbatim. Often it is not correctly capitalized, which you may choose to correct.
- **Deadline** – Once you accept the article by pressing the "I want to write this article" button, you have this much time to submit it. See the discussion of other types of deadlines in a later section.
- **Word Count** – This is the actual word count, not including the title. The lower number is a strict minimum. If you go over the maximum count a few to several words, it is unlikely the client will complain but try to stay at or under this number. Infrequently, you will see a single number word count instead of a range.
- **Possible Earnings** – This is simply the word count range times the per-word rate for the star-rating of the article. In this case (Figure 10), it's easy to calculate since 3-star orders pay one cent per word.
- **Client ID** – This is the anonymous idea of the client. It's clickable. Follow the link and you can see/set a specific Direct

Order rate for the client, see their historical revision rate or send them a message if you have a question about the order.
- **Required Keywords** – These are the primary keywords and their required frequency. I discuss in detail the ins and outs of keywords in a subsequent chapter as this is an area that can easily bog down your work if you are not careful.
- **Countdown** – This 10-minute timer shows the amount of time you have left to make a decision about accepting or deferring on this order. The countdown is a bit trickier than it appears at first glance, so its description has its own section … **next**.

The 10-Minute Open Order Timer

Being able to rapidly digest the contents of an Open Order is important because you have a limited time to peruse all the information it displays.

As soon as you open it, a 10-minute timer starts, which you can see at the Countdown field near the top of the order. Let's not dwell on the possible reasons that Textbroker wants to limit how long you can look at an Open Order, but simply accept it as such and what it means to you.

Textbroker refers to this time as the "Preview Lock" because while you are looking at the order it is removed from the Open Orders list temporarily. In other words, only you can see it while you have it open and before the timer runs out.

During that initial 10 minutes, you can choose to accept the order, reject the order or simply close/cancel the order page. Obviously, if you accept it, you are on the hook to deliver that article before the stated deadline. If you reject it, you will never see that order again. It disappears from your view of the pool.

During this first 10-minute viewing interval, if you close/cancel the page, almost nothing happens. The order will still be viewable by you in the pool.

I say "almost" because there is a side effect after all. That's because you only get two shots at viewing any specific Open Order and closing it (or letting the timer run out) uses one of those shots.

If you open the same order a second time any time later, that 10-minute timer starts up again but not at 10 minutes. Instead it begins counting from the time left at your last viewing. You can accept or reject the order or close the page just like before.

However, this time if you close the page (or let the timer run out) that order will no longer be available for you to view. The effect in this case is identical to rejecting the order.

Client Briefing

The briefing section below the top half of an order is where clients can provide additional instructions in free form. These instructions can be a few words to the short novel provided in the order highlighted in Figure 11 below. Client instruction contents often clarify their desires for the article, provide references, article outline or additional keywords. Secondary keywords especially have potential to trip you up, so are covered in detail in a subsequent chapter.

Things to Look Out for Before Accepting an Open Order

Before you become a Direct Order author exclusively, you are going to have to deal with the Open Order pool. I've already discussed the benefits it provides and it is a good idea to keep these in mind as there will be times when OOs produce frustration and threaten to drain any enthusiasm you had for learning copywriting. So, let's look at a few characteristics of "bad" Open Orders that can drive you batty and create unnecessary work for you. You will quickly learn to avoid these and move on to more profitable OOs.

Short Word Counts

Regardless of the length of any order, there is a certain fixed overhead cost beyond actually writing it. This overhead includes the time to read and evaluate the order, organizing your thoughts and research plus the time it takes to submit and order.

The longer the word count, in general, the smaller percentage of your total time is taken up by this overhead. A good rule of thumb to avoid letting overhead eat too deeply into your hourly rate, choose orders of at least 300 words over those that are shorter all else being equal.

Chapter 8 – Deciphering TB Orders

Especially during the U.S. holiday season, you will see a lot of orders (mainly for product descriptions) with word counts of 50-75 words or even less. You will spend about as much time on the "overhead" for these as you will writing them. If they can be written in cookie-cutter fashion however (without copying), then they can be profitable.

Despite what I just said, when you are just starting out do not overly concern yourself with article length. It is far more important to try as many topics, formats and article lengths as you can to get a feel for what kinds of articles are going to make you the most money in the shortest time. But, as you gain experience, try to give more weight in your Open Order evaluations to larger word counts.

Overly Specific or Tedious Instructions

Many Open Order instructions are brief and to the point. They essentially give you the topic area, the tone they are looking for, maybe one or two easily integrated keywords and a link or two to reference articles. That is all a good writer should require.

However, I'd say that around a fifth of Open Orders go completely overboard on providing instructions that go on and on in compulsive detail. For a short article of, say, 300 words, it is going to take you as much time to digest those instructions as it will to actually write the piece.

This snippet in Figure 11 of just the client instructions from one Open Order illustrates this point neatly. The instructions are 1,677 words long and will take you as much time to absorb as it probably will to write the article.

Chapter 8 – Deciphering TB Orders

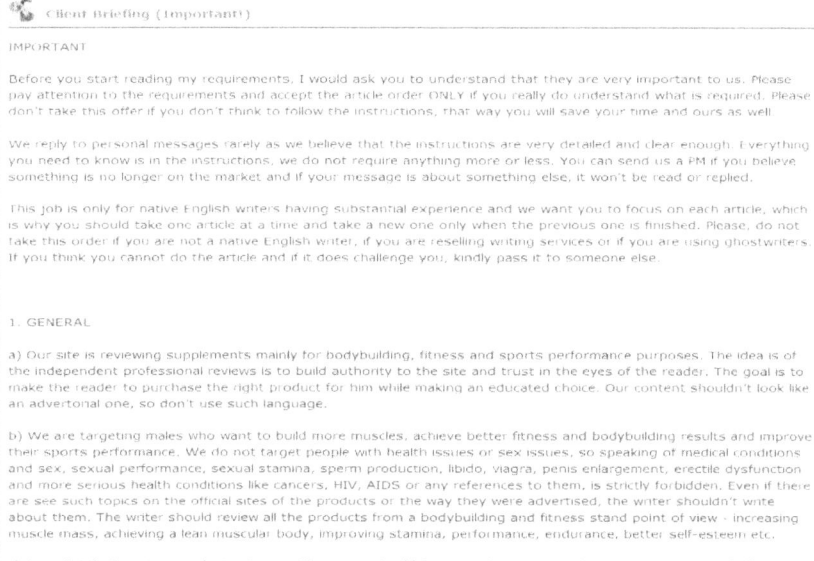

Figure 11 - Example of Too Much Detail That Spells Trouble (1,677 words total!)

Not only can client instructions such as these be long and tedious, they often ask for far more in-depth research than is appropriate, especially at Open Order prices.

My cynical theory as to why clients go overboard like this is that since they are not paying little they expect mediocre writers that require hand-holding to raise the quality.

To me, this is penny-wise and pound-foolish, but it is what it is and apparently they do find writers willing to accept such orders. However, if you can find other articles in the pool with terser instructions, all other things equal, go for those instead.

An exception to this red flag is when there are a large number of orders from the same client with more or less identical instructions. In that case, you will have these instructions memorized after writing 2 or 3 articles, which will make the remainder go much faster.

Deadlines

There are actually several types of deadlines when you are writing for Textbroker:

Chapter 8 – Deciphering TB Orders

- The deadline for submission once you have accepted an article, which is stated at the top of the order as "Deadline:" This is expressed usually as one to 10 days depending on article length. This is also known as a **processing deadline**. See Figure 12 below. The processing deadline is circled at the top.
- A **drop-dead deadline**, if any, may be expressed by the client within the instructions. For instance, even though an order was submitted on the 10th of the month with a processing deadline of two days, it may not actually be needed until the 15th. The latter is the drop-dead or hard deadline. The example order in Figure 12 below circles such a hard date within the instructions.
- The **pool deadline** is a new feature that Textbroker recently added for clients. It is an optional expiration time/date for the *existence* of the order. In other words, it tells you how long until the order is pulled from the pool. You will not see it on all orders.
- If the client does not specify a drop-dead deadline in the instructions, then you can, within reason, make up your own **soft deadline**. This tactic helps little with pool orders as there is usually someone else to pick up an order on which you defer. For Direct Orders, if it is the weekend or my current work queue is full, I often delay acceptance of an order so that the submission deadline clock does not start ticking when I have no time to work on it.

If you decide to defer picking up a Direct Order for a couple of days and the client has not specified a drop-dead deadline, drop them a note acknowledging the order and when you expect to pick it up. It is rare, but they might indicate that they need it right away, in which case you might have to squeeze it in or refuse the order.

Chapter 8 – Deciphering TB Orders

Figure 12 - Example of Processing and Drop-Dead Deadlines

By the way, I consider the instructions in the example Open Order above ("Best Kitchens", Figure 12) to be ideal. Guidance is brief but complete, a reference link is included and the tone is friendly. An experienced writer will appreciate the freedom such an order grants to concentrate on writing an engaging article without excessive oversight.

High Revision Rate

When you click on the Client ID in any order, a new page appears that displays the client's request for revision rate. Most clients have a revision rate of less than one percent. When the rate is three percent or higher, I recommend you avoid that client. Three revision requests out of a hundred might sound miniscule, but it always seems that they issue revision requests to *you* at a higher rate.

Most revision requests are simple to fulfill, but must be submitted within 24 hours. If they are asking for changes to the writing style or significant content modifications, these eat into your hourly rate.

A high revision rate plus overly detailed article instructions spell double-trouble. The client's revision rate who wrote those long instructions above, for example, was 4.17 percent and I would, based on experience, treat that order as if it was contagious.

Condescending Tone

Some clients write their orders in a bossy manner. They shout at you in all caps, imply they will blacklist you if your article is not original or violated one of their many rules. Even worse, in my opinion, they dangle the carrot of additional orders if they like your writing. How they will do that in the OO pool is beyond me.

I find that such condescending communications from clients instills in me the urge to look for orders elsewhere.

Keyword Trouble

Many Open Orders do not specify keywords, but those that do should give you a minute's pause for thought to make sure they will not paint you into a corner. I'll cover the pitfalls of keywords in much more detail in Chapter 9, but at the least imagine using the keywords in complete sentences to see if they will fall in place without you having to bend over backwards to make them flow naturally in the text.

Only a Few Orders in a Category

This red flag may seem arbitrary, but "lone" orders are potentially troublesome. If you see only one to three orders in a particular category, there is likely a good reason they have been passed up. This is especially true if the OO pool in general has few orders at that moment.

Chapter 8 – Deciphering TB Orders

There are various reasons these orders could be "bad" and it is not always obvious why. Often the instructions are very unclear or they contain keywords that must be "hammered" into place. Look these lone wolves over carefully for potential trouble before accepting them.

Chapter 9 – Unlocking the Mysteries of Keywords

The keywords section of any order is critical. However, it may add unwanted complexity to your order, which I will endeavor to explain. Keyword parsing can get quite complicated, so I'm sure to miss the more subtle cases, but what we cover here solves 95 percent of the problems you may encounter.

Many articles longer than 200 words typically request one up to several required keywords. These are part of the article's SEO as determined by the client, which is one aspect that helps an article rise in search engine rankings. The "density" of these keywords is critical. Too few instances and it ranks low for that keyword. Too many and the search engine may knock its ranking down to punish it for "keyword stuffing."

In the first example Open Order presented in Chapter 8, there is only a single keyword phrase (Richard Blair), which should pose no problems. You would simply include this name within your article at least three times and no more than five times as specified in the order. That is the simplest case.

When you copy your text into the submission section (more on that in a later chapter), Textbroker automatically scans your article for required keywords or key phrases and counts them. If any count is off, you will be unable to submit the article without editing the problem by either adding or removing specific keywords.

Chapter 9 – Unlocking the Mysteries of Keywords

Keyword Difficulties

Here are several situations where you may run into time-consuming problems with keywords.

Awkward Phrasing

Thankfully, most keywords or keyword phrases are nouns and thus they are easy to incorporate into the text. For instance, "online business opportunities" is a noun phrase that will fit naturally into your text three or more times even in a short article without jarring the reader.

However, since many required keywords in article orders are derived from using an online tool such as Google AdSense, the clients sometimes pull the phrases derived by these tools verbatim without thinking about how they would be used in a normal English sentence.

Take for instance the phrase "light bar jeep cherokee." This is just the sort of backwards phrase (a noun followed by an adjective) that anyone might type into a smart Internet search engine that is smart enough to sort out unordered words to produce useable results. However, making the exact phrase fit naturally into a sentence is extremely tough. Try it and see what you come up with.

Sometimes, the client helps you out by specifying that connecting words or inflections of the keyword may be used, which provides some leeway. In that case, you could use "light bar *for a* Jeep Cherokee" where "for" and "a" are connecting words. Otherwise, you will waste time thinking of solutions such as "A *light bar Jeep Cherokee* enthusiasts love is the 20-inch bar."

OK, we got out of that one, but now consider this key phrase: "mounting 30 led bar roof" which is an actual example from an order I received. I can't think of a solution for that one, but maybe you can?

By the way, letter case in keywords does not matter, so you can always modify capitalization as needed without changing keyword matching.

Chapter 9 – Unlocking the Mysteries of Keywords

What to do in the face of brain-teaser keywords:

- Work them in as best as you can. If your article is chosen for review, the reviewers take into account the instructions and are apt to let it pass.
- Ask the client to enable the use of connecting words or inflections. However, this will delay work on the order and may annoy the client, so only do this if nothing else works.
- Completely intractable keywords may be added to the bottom of the article in square brackets, which satisfies the keyword counter and lets TB reviewers know of your difficulty.

Secondary Keyword Issues

At times, clients include a list of secondary keywords in order instructions. These likely came from a Google AdSense keyword search. These rarely have a required count and, in my opinion, are optional. I've skipped the worst offenders without any client complaints so far.

A peculiar problem with secondary keywords comes about when they overlap with primary keywords, which throws off your primary keyword count because the Textbroker system cannot distinguish them from primary keywords. This problem can be tough to track down if you have not experienced it.

Here is a simple example to illustrate this point:

Primary keywords are "rugged boat fenders", "boat fenders", and "polyester boat fender". Secondary keywords are "polyester boat fenders", "plastic boat fenders", and "rubber boat fenders".

Although the first two primary keywords overlap, the TB system distinguishes between them. However, all three secondary keywords (which were listed in the instructions) overlap with "boat fenders" and will increment the primary keyword count. If "boat fenders" is supposed to occur only twice in the article, then you cannot include all three of those secondary keywords or you will exceed the keyword limit.

If keyword overlap is a common problem with a particular client, send them a gently-worded explanation about the problems you are seeing

Chapter 9 – Unlocking the Mysteries of Keywords

along with examples. They will appreciate this as most have no knowledge of how the TB keyword system works on the writer's side.

Chapter 10 - Team Orders and Expert Teams

Team Orders

Team Orders differ from Open Orders in a few ways:

- Unlike a simple Open Order category, Team Orders are focused more tightly around a specific topic
- You only see the actual orders if you are a member of the team but the team invitation typically has a good deal of description about what topics are offered
- They usually pay a bit more than Open Orders, sometimes a lot more, but less than what you can charge for Direct Orders
- The teams when managed by a Textbroker staff member are termed "managed teams."

A managed team relieves the client from the tedium of creating detailed orders for each article they wish to order. A staff member collects all the information for the client, places the orders (on a separate Team Orders page) and occasionally they try to drive the team's enthusiasm a bit higher when orders are not picked up quickly enough. The only other characteristic of Team Orders different than Open Orders is that the mandatory article acceptance time is often a day or two longer than for Open Orders. Otherwise, the orders themselves look just like any other.

The great thing about Team Orders besides their higher rates is that there is absolutely no penalty for joining any team and never writing a single article for it. Thus, there is great incentive to join as many teams as you like. Some teams will specify a certain star level and most ask for a brief (50 to 100 words) sample of your writing however.

Chapter 10 - Team Orders and Expert Teams

Besides team invitations, there is a pool of open teams that you can join anytime. These are called Casting Call Teams (see Figure 13 below). You will see them under the Team Orders menu item at the top of your home page. Sometimes, you see seemingly outrageous word rates (e.g., upwards of 10 cents per word) but those have strict expertise requirements. I personally think a number of those with high rates are fishy because I have gained admission to a few but never saw a single order proffered.

Team Name	Assignments	authors	Date created	Client ID	Price per word	Hide Team
Blog Team	219	852	01/23/2013	2145561	1.37 cents	
4-Star Exciting Team	189	1444	01/31/2014	2134413	2.10 cents	
Microsite Copy	174	10	09/21/2016	2460423	1.63 cents	
Health Insurance	72	34	07/16/2014	2003881	2.01 cents	
Car Insurance Info	57	70	07/01/2014	2003881	2.28 cents	
Coupon Companies	55	625	04/23/2014	2262081	1.56 cents	
AD Misc SG	39	416	02/24/2015	2354201	1.95 cents	
Shopping Savers	18	252	05/20/2015	2262081	1.95 cents	
Netmark	16	142	12/13/2012	2176757	1.54 cents	
Life Insurance Info	14	22	07/16/2014	2003881	2.01 cents	
AD Misc	12	292	02/24/2015	2354889	1.95 cents	
Training 1	12	372	05/14/2015	2373625	1.56 cents	
HVAC Rapid Dev Team	10	37	11/08/2012	2123712	8.45 cents	
Med Writers	6	67	01/18/2016	2413605	1.56 cents	
Home Insurance Info	6	26	07/16/2014	2003881	2.01 cents	
Five Star Writers	6	24	04/29/2016	2419045	2.28 cents	
City Security	6	2	10/28/2016	2455093	1.56 cents	
Homestead WebContent	3	68	12/26/2012	2005583	1.75 cents	

Figure 13 - Besides Team Invitations Open Casting Calls Offer Thousands of Opportunities

Expert Teams

These teams are a special class of the TB team concept. Think of them as the Team Order Elite Core. Only 4- or 5-star writers are allowed into these teams plus the selection process is stricter than for regular teams. Textbroker staff say who gets to be on an Expert Team and they solicit members by direct invitation only.

Another unique aspect to Expert Teams is that their topic area is industry-specific within which they may specialize. Each team will have

Chapter 10 - Team Orders and Expert Teams

its own mini-landing site from which orders are issued and the team has a single per word rate set by Textbroker. Naturally, they pay more than regular Team Orders with an average of 5c to 10c per word, so they could be lucrative if you can land an invitation.

Chapter 11 - Direct Orders

The attainment of Direct Orders at the 4-star level should be your guiding mission from the day you join Textbroker. Forgive me if I continue to drive that point. For the last two years, I have written DOs exclusively on Textbroker and enjoy my Textbroker experience, despite some shortcomings of their site, more than ever.

Why the Focus on DOs?

- You will make more money guaranteed. You will be in control of your per-word rate in general and per client.
- Your writing will be more closely aligned with your interests and expertise. Writing about things you know well is the most enjoyable form of writing I know.
- You develop a rapport with your clients that is missing in Open or Team Orders via closer collaboration with the client.
- Typically, DOs from a specific client follow a particular topic area (e.g., blog posts for a cloud technology company), which naturally builds your expertise in their sector. That makes subsequent articles easier, faster and more profitable to write.
- Positive client evaluations are far more common with DO clients than others. These evaluations are separate from your star rating but do carry some weight with TB when they perform periodic evaluations. Even if TB did not consider them, they are worthwhile as invigorating mood boosters, which any copywriter needs now and then.

Chapter 11 - Direct Orders

The Mechanics of DOs

When you set up your profile, you will see a field where you can set your Direct Order rate. I recommend setting this right from the start at 2 cents per word. That's already over a 40 percent raise over a 4-star Open Order rate. Pat yourself on the back.

However, do not expect DOs to start flowing in right away. This is where that double-edged sword of minimal marketing responsibility within TB cuts the other way. In other words, you have a limited ability to market your writing skills to clients who want to make Direct Orders.

What marketing ability you have comes via profile writing samples, direct messages with potential clients and the work you accomplish in the Open Order pool. Mostly you have to wait for clients to find you, but you can add the potential to net a DO client when evaluating which Open Orders you pick up.

Nevertheless, once you get to a 4-star quality level (and possibly at three stars), probes from potential DO clients do being to show up in your messages inbox. Expect to see DO inquiries after a few months if your writing samples display expertise in a hot area such as technology, law, health or business.

Direct Order Format

Refer to the Open Orders chapter to see how Direct Orders look, since they use an identical format. Besides the standard TB order form, some DO clients use off-TB documents via a link to a Google Drive file or something similar. I assume they have special dispensation from Textbroker as TB normally does not like outside links to be used in client communications.

These documents are typically spreadsheets with a list of article titles along with some research links or specific instructions. If I'm writing a series of articles for a DO client that uses of one these docs, I open it in a separate tab and pin it in my browser for reference over the week or two it usually takes to complete the list.

Chapter 11 - Direct Orders

A Note about Setting Client Rates

Here is an important final word about article per-word rates. Always bear in mind that the rate you charge is not the same rate that the client sees. Whatever the article rate is that you set, Textbroker adds an additional 35 percent to that on the client side. For example, if your DO rate is 4 cents per word, the client will see 5.4 cents per word on his or her side of the garden wall when they look at your profile.

I am tempted to discuss the merits and demerits of that 35% commission, which as a writer I think is on the high side, but it is what it is. In fact, do not be surprised if in the future, as in the past, they raise it.

The important thing about this additional 35 percent is that the vast majority of clients are completely unaware of it. Thus, you need to exercise a bit of care discussing your rates in direct messages between yourself and them. Mentioning your rate may occur when a client first contacts you or during a time when you are adjusting your rate up or down and want to inform current and past clients.

You could discuss your rate in one of two ways. Either state the rate paid to you plus mention that TB is going to add 35 percent to that, or calculate the total on your side and tell them the full client rate only. I prefer the former approach because it makes it clear that the full price is not all due to you and because it avoids either side making a mathematical error.

There is a positive side to the seemingly large commission TB charges. It tells you what the market is actually willing to pay for your work should you ever decide to seek writing jobs outside of Textbroker.

Chapter 12 - Your First Writing Jobs

First-Time Jitters

If you have little experience in writing in exchange for money, you may be a bit nervous when taking on your early articles. This derives from being subject to judgment from both the client and those persnickety TB editors. If you followed the guidelines provided in the section "Things to Look Out for Before Accepting an Open Order" in Chapter 8, then it is unlikely you will hear anything critical from clients plus they are more likely to leave you a positive Client Evaluation, if they leave one at all.

The TB proofreaders will check and rate your first five articles and subsequent articles periodically to see if you are still writing at your star level or if you deserve a promotion or demotion. But, as I pointed out earlier, take these as constructive criticism. They really are trying to help even if the evaluations seem a bit cold.

Focus on Open and Team Orders

Everyone starts with Open Orders and you should expect these to be the bulk of your work for a few months at least. Start off with OO topics with which you already have experience, but make a point of occasionally stretching yourself to take on topics that require additional research. The more topics you can bring into your writing comfort zone, the more work you will have and the more opportunities for Direct Orders you create.

Chapter 12 - Your First Writing Jobs

During downtime, peruse the Casting Call Team invitations and sign up for any that look interesting. If they pay more than your current star-level OO rate, all the better. If you receive any team invitations, always accept them as there is simply no downside to adding them to your home teams. You get access to new orders not in the OO pool, but you are not under any obligation to accept them. It's a win-win.

Prepare Yourself to Attract Direct Orders

Set a reasonable Direct Order rate in your profile of two cents per word when starting out. Try not to turn down any Direct Order work that comes your way even if it seems you are going to be spending as much time researching as writing. Direct Order experience is invaluable and well worth the extra investment of time to land them in the long run. Work on creating a broader variety of writing samples in your profile to attract more DO inquiries from new clients.

Again, stretch yourself to take on Open or Team Orders that require that you gain more expertise in new areas that can be used as writing samples.

Keep your eyes on the prize and soon you will have enough DO work that you will be able to bump up your DO per-word rate another half cent or even more if demand is good. Within a year or so, you could be charging upwards of 4 cents per word. Remember that you also have the ability to set even higher rates on a per-client basis too. If you do raise an existing client's rate, send them a courtesy message beforehand telling them why as a courtesy.

Deliver on Time

Beating deadlines always makes a positive impression on clients. Strive to get your articles done well ahead of the client's deadline (the hard or drop-dead deadline) and definitely before the submission deadline. It is embarrassing to miss a submission deadline because then you have to bother the client to resubmit the order.

Naturally, there are going to be situations where you miss a deadline. Life happens. I've dropped the ball several times due to poor estimates of my writing queue, getting sick or due to an unanticipated family

Chapter 12 - Your First Writing Jobs

emergency. Clients have always been tolerant of my misses, especially if I tell them in advance that I screwed up and cannot get their article done on time.

Drop Everything to Service a Revision Request

Revision requests are not frequent by any means, but they always irk me because it means having to revisit work that I thought was done. About half the time, they are due to my error and the other half due to faulty instructions. Very few (5%) require more than 15 minutes to clear up. So, it's best to jump on these as soon as possible and get them out of your hair. You have to keep an eye out for them in your email or TB messages inbox as you only have 24 hours to resubmit the article from the time the request was entered. Fortunately, they almost always show up within a day or two of submitting the original article, so if they have not come in by then you probably will not see one.

Communicating with Clients

The primary way you have of communicating with clients is via the Textbroker messaging system (albeit some clients send a link to off-site instructions). Textbroker monitors the messages between you and the client on their site. They are looking for the potential to breach their client-author firewall with mentions of information that may identify you or external links that a client might follow that lead to the same sort of personally identifiable information. So, keep their justified paranoia in mind.

When talking with clients, keep your messages on-point and brief. Try not to add extraneous information unrelated to the writing task. Avoid being overly chatty but keep it friendly. If client questions or instructions are ambiguous, do not hesitate to ask for clarification in a follow-up message.

Article Evaluations

When I first started writing for Textbroker, I was a bit put off by their written evaluations of my work. That is not because I had an issue with their corrections, which were spot on. Their staff are highly trained

Chapter 12 - Your First Writing Jobs

proofreaders and have years more experience in writing than I do. I respect that.

However, their evaluations are delivered in an almost robotic tone that can be misinterpreted easily as condescension by novice writers. Furthermore, if you write a perfect article without spelling or grammar errors, all you get back for your evaluation is "Well done," which is nice though not terribly inspiring.

If I'm honest, what truly gets my goat about these written evaluations is how many times I make the same set of mistakes before I finally get a particular grammar rule through my thick skull. It is even worse than that, since they include clear examples of the right way to avoid a particular error in their evaluations, so I have no excuse the next time.

By the way, Textbroker changed their evaluation process in June 2016. It used to be that they infrequently rated a batch of five articles at once and determined your average star rating from those. Now, they evaluate single articles but more frequently. Do not dread these evaluations but rather look forward to them as they keep your writing skills on track.

What If Your Star Level Is Reduced?

If their evaluations result in knocking you down a star level, do not despair.

The things to do if this happens are to:

1) Review your mistakes and look up the relevant rules online so you can avoid them in your next articles,

2) Quickly write another five articles and as soon as clients accept them

3) Email authors@textbroker.com asking for a re-evaluation based on those five articles. Hopefully, you proofread those articles thoroughly and either corrected errors or re-wrote sentences into simpler sentences to avoid a grammar issue you may not fully grasp.

A lot of TB authors do not realize they can ask for expedited re-evaluations and continue to write articles at a lower star level waiting for the time when the proofreaders get to them, which could be months. Sadly, they miss out on higher pay during that time.

Chapter 12 - Your First Writing Jobs

Making Money Is the Name of the Game

When writing at a per-word rate, time is of the essence. The faster you can crank out solid copy, the more money you will make. Many of the tips presented in this book are aimed at helping you to become as efficient in writing TB content as possible. Writing fast comes naturally if you write a lot, so write as often as possible. You will develop a rhythm to your work as your experience grows.

Chapter 13 - Tips on Becoming a Profitable Copywriter

Familiarizing Yourself with Topics

Writing is like public speaking in that it works best if you already have personal experience with the topic. Your experience allows you to impart information in a natural manner, which increases your connection to the reader or listener as the case may be. Especially if you are a new copywriter, choosing topics with which you already have at least passing familiarity builds confidence. Gradually, branch out to other topic areas and supplement your knowledge with research either online or by talking to people with relevant know-how.

Speed is King for Per-Word Orders

I'm sure that there are many authors who write twice as fast as I average, but my goal is 500 words per hour. This requires concentration and staying in the chair for at least 30-minute stretches. Depending on the nature of the article (long, short, technical or not, etc.), my per-hour rate varies from 300 words up to 1,000 word. At my current DO rates, that is between $12 up to $40 per hour, but mostly I average between $15 and $25 an hour.

Gaining speed takes experience and practicing good writing habits such as outlining your article before writing it. It is a *lot* easier to set up your sub-headings and then write five 100-word sections versus trying to write a 500 word article all at once. Another hindrance to speed is the understandable urge to produce perfect sentences on the first pass. I recommend you approach a writing task in three stages: rough draft, clean-up and proofreading. My favorite Ernest Hemingway quote, which is perfectly apropos to this concept is "The first draft of anything is shit." Essentially this boils down to write first, clean up later.

Avoid the Enemy of Done

As a writer you have a tremendous advantage over a speaker in that you can take time to correct inaccuracies and bad grammar or remove fluff and awkward phrasings. Going overboard on fine-tuning your article, however, can severely impact your hourly rate. Seeking perfection in copywriting at any level below 5-stars is going to cost you money. Try instead to realize a sense of "good enough" and know when to move on.

This is easier said than done, especially with a new Direct Order client you want to impress and you can be forgiven in that case. Otherwise, strive more for speed than having your articles strive for the New York Times Bestseller List.

And rest assured, though many articles will not invoke in you a warm, fuzzy satisfying feeling, there will be many along the way that flow like well-aged literary wine from your mind and fingertips almost without effort. Savor those.

Take the Direct Approach

New copywriters being paid by the word are often tempted, often unconsciously, to ramble in their writing, which produces a higher word count but negatively impacts clarity and leaves the reader impatiently anticipating your point.

For short orders, such as product descriptions, this habit is anathema to the task at hand. But, even for longer orders, you will impress your clients and avoid time-wasting revisions if you strive to produce clear, direct and succinct writing.

Get to the point of the article in the first sentence if possible without "introducing" the topic. When writing and especially when reviewing your work, look for simpler ways to express facts, thoughts and conclusions. If you can say the same thing in one or two 10-word sentences or three longer sentences, choose the former. Break up run-on sentences, which also have a tendency to present grammar problems anyway.

Overcoming Writer's Block

Most people envision a writer in anguish, head in hands, leaning over a blank piece of paper or a blank computer monitor when they think of writer's block. Ninety-nine percent of the time, however, it is far more subtle than that. It usually boils down to procrastination fed by an anxious feeling that you are not up to the task of writing a coherent article of a few hundred words. You are probably nowhere near your keyboard when this is happening.

The voice in your head will be saying "Well, that article will only take a couple of hours at most and the deadline isn't until tomorrow …" or other rationalizations of that kind. You will find a dozen other things, great and small, that you feel you must complete in order to "prepare" or "clear the decks." Only then, you tell yourself, will you be able to give that article the concentration it deserves.

All mental acrobatics actually accomplish, however, is to decrease the time available to write said article, which further increases your anxiety to the point that the only way to relieve it is to finally do the work. Meanwhile, you have stressed yourself out, and it is more than likely that your writing suffers for it.

I could write a book on the topic of writer's block, but you can just as easily research the topic online. I suffer from it too and despite knowing it is happening and how it impedes my work, it is not easy to defeat at times. So, certainly I do not have all the answers when combatting this demon.

All I can say is that the best technique that works for me is to force myself to write … anything … for only 10 minutes and no more. I promise myself that even if it comes out as total crapola, it is OK. Far more often than not, those few minutes are all I need to break through the block and "prime the pump." Before I know it, a half-hour or even an

Chapter 13 - Tips on Becoming a Profitable Copywriter

hour flies by before I've glanced at the time and a first draft is well underway.

Never Stop Learning

This book recommends that you strive to be a Textbroker 4-star writer. There is good money and lots of work at that level. You do not have to be a literature major nor have perfect grammar to achieve and maintain that level. As you gain confidence, your enjoyment of writing and your writing will both improve.

It is easy to become complacent at that point and slackening your learning pace compared to when you started copywriting is only natural. However, the best recipe for continued success is to make a habit out of continuing to improve your understanding of grammar and attempting techniques to write more effectively and efficiently. Try this: spend just 15 minutes a day, every day, looking up a point of grammar, reviewing the AP Style Guide or reading a post on your favorite writing blog.

As you absorb more writing skills bit by bit, plan to review your Textbroker writing samples every couple of weeks and see if you can apply what you have learned to those.

Writing samples are invaluable for obtaining new Direct Order clients, so the sharper they are the better. Plus, you are not under a deadline when working on those, so you can really dig into them, perhaps rewriting them in their entirety.

Chapter 14 - Writing Resources

Grammar References

- Adverbial Clause – Memorize this important point of grammar, you will use it often [https://en.wikipedia.org/wiki/Adverbial_clause#Kinds_of_adverbial_clauses]
- Purdue Writing Lab Coordinating Conjunctions – Likewise, memorize, especially FANBOYS [https://owl.english.purdue.edu/engagement/3/4/76/]
- Purdue Writing Lab Use of Commas – AP Style leaves out the final comma before "and" in Rule 5 [https://owl.english.purdue.edu/owl/resource/607/02/]

Writing Guides

- Purdue Professional Writing Articles – Lots of good stuff here, use these as continuing education [https://owl.english.purdue.edu/owl/resource/681/01/]
- The Editors' Guide to Article Writing for Newbies – Must-read covering the fundamentals of good copywriting [http://thoughtcatalog.com/kamilia-khairul-anuar/2013/08/the-editors-guide-to-article-writing-for-newbies/]
- English Grammar Writing Guides – Covers essential grammar topics [http://www.englishgrammar.org/writing-guides/]
- A Step-by-Step Guide to Writing a Compelling Article Introduction – Since many writers get stuck here (as well as in the article conclusion), this is essential

- [https://www.quicksprout.com/2016/07/25/a-step-by-step-guide-to-writing-a-compelling-article-introduction/]
- The Textbroker Blog – Has dozens of articles for authors about all aspects of copywriting on Textbroker for both authors and clients [https://www.textbroker.com/blog/author]

Tools

Plagiarism Checkers

- Plagiarisma.net [http://plagiarisma.net/]
- Plagramm [https://www.plagramme.com/]
- Plagium [http://www.plagium.com/]
- CopyGator [http://www.copygator.com/]

Capitalization Checkers

- CapitalizeMyTitle – My favorite, covers all style guides [http://capitalizemytitle.com/]
- Headline Capitalization – Covers various styles plus good explanations of the rules [https://headlinecapitalization.com/]

Miscellaneous, Interesting Copywriting Related Resources

- AP Style Guard – This is a non-free Word plug-in that may improve your productivity [http://www.apstylebook.com/?do=product&pid=style-guard]
- 101 Copywriting Dos and Don'ts – Informative and amusing to boot [http://copyhackers.com/downloads/worksheets/Copy-Hackers-101-Copywriting-Dos-and-Don%27ts.pdf]
- Grammar Girl – Entertaining variety of grammar tips with fresh content [http://www.quickanddirtytips.com/grammar-girl]
- How to Improve the Clarity of Your Writing – Discusses the Flesch-Kincaid Grading Scale and how to optimize the score for Web content [http://www.awaionline.com/2007/12/clarity-of-your-writing/]
- The Definitive Guide to Copywriting – Includes guidance on all kinds of copywriting [https://www.quicksprout.com/the-definitive-guide-to-copywriting/]

Chapter 14 - Writing Resources

- Emotional Marketing Value Headline Analyzer – Not sure how effective this is, but it is fun to use [http://www.aminstitute.com/headline/]
- Writers' Tax Deductions – At Textbroker, you work as an independent contractor. You are responsible for paying taxes on your gross income, but these deductions can significantly reduce your tax bill. [http://www.nolo.com/legal-encyclopedia/tax-deductions-writers.html]

Other Copywriting Brokers

WriterAccess – Have writer levels from 2 to 6 with per-word rates from 1.4c/word up to 7c/word, respectively but they take 30% as commission from those rates. [https://www.writeraccess.com/apply-writer/]

IWriter – As large as Textbroker with one to four star article ratings from 0.7c/word up to 7c/word from which they take a commission from the writer. They offer article re-write and eBook orders also. [https://www.iwriter.com/]

Chapter 15 - Textbroker Quirks

HTML Translation

Word Count for Plain Text vs. HTML Articles

Clients can request articles in either plain text or HTML format. If they do not specify which format they prefer in the order, it is usually safe to assume they want plain text. For Direct Order clients, I always ask if they do not specify however. The difference to them is that the HTML tags add to your article's final word count by 10 to 20% typically. You won't know the exact word count for an HTML article until you submit it in the Textbroker submission tool.

Submitting an HTML Formatted Article

You do not have to know HTML in order to create an HTML formatted document ... usually. Simply use the built-in headings, hyperlinking, bullets, etc. in Microsoft Word as you write the article. Calculate in your head coming up about 10% short on the word count before submission.

When you submit the article, instead of pasting the text into the TB submission window/editor, click on the little folder with the Word "W" symbol on it (see Figure 14 below). A new editing window will pop up into which you paste your Word doc. This widget mostly understands HTML and converts Word's headings, etc. into HTML tags.

HTML Pitfalls

I said "mostly" in that last sentence because Textbroker's HTML conversion is buggy in a couple of ways. It generally works all-right for simple articles. That is, if you only have headings, sub-headings, bullets and hyperlinks. Start going beyond that with, say, a table or form, and the output is apt to suffer a poor translation. This is especially true if a table contains fractional decimal numbers (e.g., "0.25"). In the latter case, unwanted tags are inserted, which messes up your table.

The only way to correct such errors is to manually edit the article, HTML and all, in Textbroker's none-too-generous simple editor. I know HTML well and believe me it is a royal pain in the ass to do this. If you do not know HTML, you are going to be lost and cursing the day you took my advice to sign up with Textbroker the first time you have to submit with complex HTML.

HTML Preview Formatting

Another quirk (I'd say it's a bug in their software) is how an HTML formatted document is rendered in the preview window. This is the window where you get your last chance to proof your article before either submitting it or editing it some more. With plain text this is OK. It should look the same as your plain text Word version (with the exception of paragraph breaks, see the section after this one about that).

Chapter 15 - Textbroker Quirks

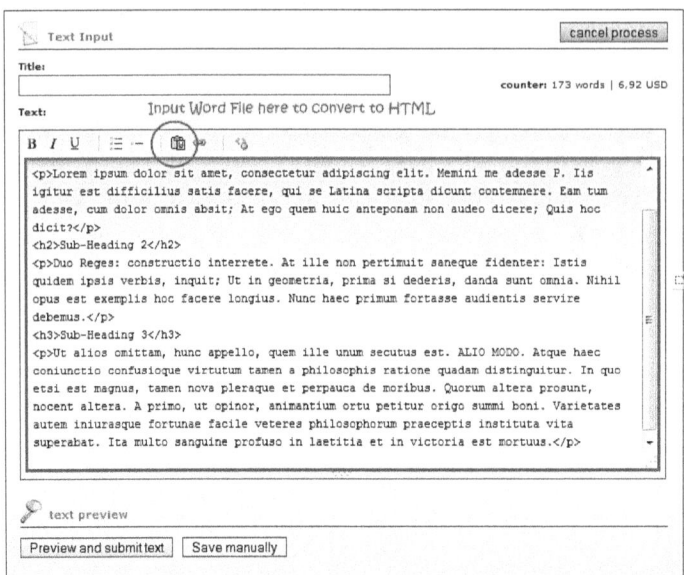

Figure 14 - Insert Word Rich Formatted Text via the TB Word Widget Popup

In Figure 14 above, text copied from a Word document using Word heading formats was input by selecting the Word widget (circled in the figure) and pasting the formatted text into the widget's popup box.

The gripe I have is with how TB's HTML rendering treats headings and sub-headings. Specifically, as you can see in the snapshot below (Figure 15), it colors headings and sub-headings differently and displays sub-headings with a larger font size than the main headings. It just looks strange and I've alerted a few clients to this lest they think I am the one who screwed up, although none so far seem to be bothered by it.

Chapter 15 - Textbroker Quirks

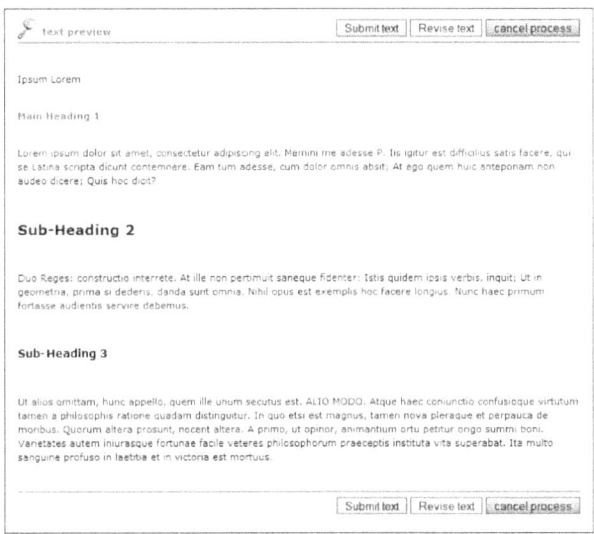

Figure 15 - How Word Rich Headings Come Out via TB's HTML Renderer

Plain Text Formatting, Preview and Editing

As I alluded to above, plain text cut-n-paste into Textbroker's submission window is relatively straightforward. However, I've found that I must insert an extra paragraph break (i.e., hit the Return key an extra time). If I do not, when the plain text is rendered for preview there is no space between paragraphs at all. Perhaps there is some setting in Word that works around this, but I don't know what that would be.

The other thing about article submission that irks me is why TB cannot make a larger submission window. There's simply no reason for this that I can see. The stingy size makes it difficult, especially if you need to navigate the window to make a few quick tweaks. It feels to me like trying to use an old VT100 monitor back in the day of mainframes (there, I've dated myself!).

Order Vanishes After Submission

Once you submit an article, the original order is no longer available to you. I've thought about why TB would do this and I cannot come up with reasonable explanations other than paranoia or oversight. Nine times out

Chapter 15 - Textbroker Quirks

of ten it is not a big deal, but there are instances where I would like to refer back to that article order for one reason or another. You could get into the habit of cutting and pasting each order you accept and saving it locally, but unless you are hyper-organized already (I'm not) that just unnecessarily adds to your writing overhead and clutter.

Tallying Your Orders and Payments

As an ex-software engineer, it always bothers me when organizations do not take advantage of the technology at their fingertips either out of ignorance or stinginess. A case in point are the tables in Textbroker that display the status of articles you have written and the payout table. These are nice to have, but they do not go far enough. They are simply raw, non-interactive lists output from their database.

When I see my articles status page, I would like to also instantly tally my earnings for the last month, quarter or year, but the only way to do that is tediously cutting and pasting the table rows into a spreadsheet. Even that is not straightforward because re-formatting is needed to remove extraneous columns and to eliminate the *trailing* dollar sign they put after pay amounts.

You should be able to see metrics such as the number of client reviews you've received, the number of revisions you've done, average article word length, etc., etc. These types of flexible views are precisely what database technology was made for.

Chapter 16 - Getting Help

The FAQ, Forum and Email

It goes without saying that you should explore the Textbroker site thoroughly, especially their FAQ and the blog. You can also find the answers to common or particular questions in the Authors Forum, but due to its non-threaded nature, I find the Forum tedious to navigate and rarely go there for answers myself. The other way to get expert advice is simply to shoot off an email to authors@textbroker.com. They typically send a reply within 12 hours though their deadline is 24 hours.

Textbroker University

When I first started writing for TB, the methods just mentioned were about all I had to operate with plus outside writing resources that mainly dealt with grammar. In the last couple of years, however, Textbroker has added a wealth of content to help writers move up the star ladder more quickly and produce high-quality content. This instructional content is called Textbroker University. It consists of blog articles, tutorials and video presentations that demystify the most common writing mistakes and their solutions.

They have divided these educational materials into three levels: for new writers trying to figure out correct grammar, 3-star writers aiming for a 4-star rating and "graduate" courses for experienced 4-star TB writers who wish to pass the proofreading test, which is the first step to a 5-star rating.

Chapter 16 - Getting Help

When TB University first started, it was a small collection of videos covering the most common grammar mistakes. Now, it is much more sophisticated.

Enrollment is required, after which they evaluate your last 5 articles. Based on these evaluations they will make recommendations as to which modules will be most helpful in advancing your writing skills. This is definitely something you want to take advantage of to move up in star ratings. Once you finish the recommended modules, you ask them to evaluate your next 5 articles, which they will do promptly. This protocol could easily bump you up from 3-stars to 4-stars in a hurry.

Opening a Client Account

This tip provides you with valuable insights that make you a more effective Textbroker author and inspire empathy for clients. There is no cost to open a client account. In fact, you can use the same email address you used to open your author account. Just remember to check the client box when logging in.

Your client account allows you to compare yourself to other authors by searching on various criteria such as area of expertise, number of articles and star level. It also provides access to other authors' profiles that you can compare to your own (do not assume they are all better than yours by the way).

As a client, Textbroker will email you vouchers now and then to use against an order. You can order an entire article with one of these vouchers without cost to you. I used one to order a 2-star article just to see what I'd get. It was, frankly, laughably bad, not even worth re-writing even if I had a place to submit it to.

Chapter 17 - Moving Beyond Textbroker

Textbroker is superb for learning Web content writing and helping improve your writing abilities over time. It is easy to supplement your TB work with other non-TB online resources as well. Obviously, it is just one of dozens of ways you could earn extra income from your writing skills.

Other Ways to Make Money Copywriting

- Try other per-word content brokers (see links in Chapter 14). Once you have the hang of Textbroker, spinning up on other sites will seem easier.
- Try freelance sites such as Upwork or Freelancer. You will compete head-to-head with established writers, so you need to concentrate on marketing your skills.
- Look for long-term employment as a writer. Utilize sites such as Freelance Writing Jobs, which is a classifieds system for writing job providers. The majority are tele-commuting jobs. You will need some solid experience and writing samples to convince someone to hire you.
- Strike out on your own as a copywriter. Start by specializing in, say, blogging or a technical topic area. May I suggest two excellent Udemy courses by Len Smith to assist you in pursuit of this path: Copywriting – Become a Freelance Copywriter and Copywriting White Papers – An All Levels Strategy.
- Start a re-write service catering to non-English speakers whose websites are often in dire need of grammatical, spelling and

Chapter 17 - Moving Beyond Textbroker

organizational help to make them readable and to inspire confidence in their domain authority.

It takes a lot of work and time to establish yourself as an independent copywriter, but the monetary rewards may be much greater than the earnings on Textbroker even for 5-star writers.

Chapter 18 – Ready for the Journey

My Path

I stumbled into copywriting as a hobby. It was a good way to earn money for special projects while still sequestering personal time for other pursuits in my semi-retirement. The fact that I had control over when and how much I worked was a big plus to me. I started as a 3-star writer but was able to move up to the 4-star level within a couple of months.

My first year, I wrote less than 100 articles. Then I started receiving my first Direct Orders. The boost in pay and the more interesting topics both inspired me to further refine my craft. Eventually, I had more DOs than I wanted, so I gradually raised my DO price over several months, which brought me a little slack, although a few new clients showed up too.

Today, I work only on DOs at prices between four and five cents per word and have 700 articles (many over 5,000 words) under my belt. I probably put in about 15-20 hours per week. My per-hour rate is between $12 and $40 per hour with an average of $18 per hour overall. I could easily double my hours, but I prefer being a part-timer so that I can pursue other interests.

I feel confident that my personal path with Textbroker is typical of other new writers. Most of us start by dabbling perhaps at the 2-star or 3-star level and, if the work is enjoyable, climb to the 4-star level with a modicum of study. We then gradually move from the Open Order pool to Team Orders to Direct Orders, refining our skills, polishing our profile and creating more sophisticated writing samples along the way.

Chapter 18 – Ready for the Journey

Starting Down Your Path Now

If you have any inclination to write, then there is no reason you cannot within a year (or much less for those more ambitious than me) be making several hundred up to two thousand dollars a month copywriting in your spare time if you apply what you have learned in this book.

I firmly believe from what I've observed as a copywriter that the field is expanding rapidly and that skilled writers are in high demand. That spells steady work and increasing numbers of lucrative writing opportunities that are opening up. You do not have to write to the caliber of, say, a national magazine article either. What you are competing with is the ubiquitous amount of surprisingly poor writing on the Internet that is holding back the essential Web presence of so many companies and entrepreneurs.

Enjoy the Scenery and Tell Me How to Help

It is my sincere hope that this book provides a gateway to your own pursuit of copywriting. I have attempted to provide in-depth detail about using Textbroker as your learning and earning platform in a way that will save you countless hours of thrashing around finding the most effective and profitable paths to Web content writing.

I look forward to any questions or comments you have regarding this book. These will aid the creation of improved future editions. Just drop me a line at adullroar@tomochka.com. I typically respond within a day or two.

Thank you so much for taking the time to read this book! I wish you the very best of luck in your copywriting adventures.

Chapter 18 – Ready for the Journey

Setting Off on a New Journey

www.ingramcontent.com/pod-product-compliance
Lightning Source LLC
Chambersburg PA
CBHW061444180526
45170CB00004B/1546